KNOWING HER PLACE

KNOWING HER PLACE

Gender and the Gospels

Anne Thurston

Paulist Press
New York • Mahwah, N. J.

Published in the USA by Paulist Press
997 Macarthur Boulevard
Mahwah, New Jersey 07430 USA

Published by arrangement with Gill & Macmillan, Dublin

© Anne Thurston 1998

ISBN 0 8091 3862 X

Print origination by *Deirdre's Desktop*

CONTENTS

PREFACE

Having read English and German literature for my primary degrees I was fascinated when I first came to theology to discover literary approaches to scripture. This interest grew and was enhanced by the discovery of feminist perspectives on texts. This book marks a stage on that journey.

For the past few years I have been involved in giving workshops primarily for women's groups but also for groups of students, and for women and men involved in Renewal Courses in Ministry. These workshops and seminars have had different titles: 'Feminist Perspectives on Scripture', 'Gender and the Gospels', 'Women's Voices'. However my approach has always been similar — I have taken a text of scripture and reflected on it with the group, inviting them to read the text 'against the grain' and thus become aware of the interests guiding both the text and their own reading. We work with two sets of texts: the texts of scripture and the scripts of their own lives, seeking to be faithful to both contexts. I introduce the method and initiate a conversation which is taken up in small discussion groups.

Almost without exception my experience of such work has been exciting and energising. I have no doubt that these classic texts of scripture still speak to us in powerful and unexpected ways. A feminist perspective casts a different light and familiar texts are suddenly new and alive again. Sometimes the power in the work comes from resisting the texts; sometimes it comes through anger and pain, sometimes through joy and the release of laughter. Often it comes simply from hearing the texts in a different voice.

This practice has shaped the reflections which follow, and my hope would be that these reflections in their turn would generate further discussion so that the word continues to enliven and enrich other communities, particularly those committed to exploring the issue of gender and the place of women in the Christian community.

However, my principal justification for writing this book has been to share my own enthusiasm for this work and for these texts: they never cease to surprise and delight me.

So I am grateful to have had the opportunities to share this interest. I am also grateful for the insights which have come from conversations with several friends and colleagues. Gabrielle has read the text and been a constant source of encouragement.

A particularly enriching experience has been my collaboration with Rev. Katherine Meyer, Community Minister in Abbey Presbyterian Church, Dublin. We have given workshops together on a number of occasions in Dublin and in Belfast. We come from different traditions — Reformed and Roman Catholic — and share a common interest both in scripture and in the flourishing of women in the Christian community. Together we have attempted to develop a model of conversation with scriptural texts which opens up to a wider conversation inclusive of different voices both inside and outside the texts, and which attempts to create a praxis of mutuality in ministry. It is an experience which I value greatly and which I see as a sign of hope. To her and to all the women who may hear their voices on these pages I offer my thanks.

Thanks are also due to Jim McArdle who helped to tame an unruly text.

Finally, thank you to Tim and to our children Katie, Lucy and Dominic for the walks down the pier and the talks which sustained me — and for much, much more!

Anne Thurston
June 1998

NOTE ON ABBREVIATIONS

I have chosen to work with the New Revised Standard Version of the Bible, henceforth NRSV.
Occasionally I refer to the Revised Standard Version, RSV.

Tell the Truth but tell it slant —
Success in Circuit lies
Too bright for our infirm Delight
The Truth's superb surprise

As Lightning to the children eased
With explanation kind
The Truth must dazzle gradually
Or every man be blind —

Emily Dickinson

INTRODUCTION

'Moreover some women of our group astounded us ... Some of those who were with us went to the tomb and found it just as the women had said; but they did not see him.' Then he said to them, 'Oh how foolish you are and slow of heart to believe all that the prophets have declared! ... Then beginning with Moses and the prophets he interpreted to them all the things about himself in all the scriptures. (Luke 24: 22; 25: 27)

Recently I listened to the novelist A. S. Byatt give a talk on BBC Radio about Velasquez's painting of Jesus in the House of Mary and Martha.[1] This imaginative exploration was one of a series of 'word pictures' where authors interpreted paintings. I found myself fascinated by the process of interpretation illustrated by this project. The novelist was interpreting a painting, which in turn was an interpretation of a text, and in this process the original text became as it were doubly illuminated. I found myself considering the whole process of interpretation and the fact that this little original story could bear the weight of so much reflection! It seems clear that scriptural texts such as this one indeed merit the description 'classic texts', defined by theologian David Tracy as, 'those texts which bear an excess and permanence of meaning, yet always resist definitive interpretation'.[2] I was sharply aware of the perennial freshness of this familiar story yielding to multiple interpretations. A. S. Byatt was using the lens of a writer, a critic; Velasquez had approached the story with the eye of a painter. Byatt was interpreting not only the painting but the text seen through the eyes of the painter and then in turn through her own eyes. I was reminded of the disciples on the road to Emmaus interpreting and reinterpreting the events which had occurred.[3] To interpret experience is not an option; how we interpret is the issue.

Each interpretation frames the event, each reader — herself an interpreter — needs to be aware of the frame and to recognise that she too will frame the text. Yet this framing does not fully determine the text — there is a sense in which the classic text also resists us. It may have a surplus, an excess of meaning, but it also has a power and a claim on us which Tracy, further on in the same essay, describes as claiming or commanding our attention. The classics, he points out, resist 'the temptation to domesticate all reality'.[4] Classic texts refuse to be tamed.

It is at this point that Tracy's theory about the interpretation of classic texts intersects with a feminist perspective. The feminist interpreter is suspicious of controlled readings of texts, of readings which mask the dominance of the interpreter under an apparent cloak of objectivity. One of the tasks of feminist criticism has been to remove that cloak and to lay the interpreter bare and insist that he declare his presuppositions. The feminist reader because she is open about her interpretive stance leaves herself open to the criticism of ideological bias. In fact her vulnerability before the text is that of every reader, of every interpreter. Each of us brings a certain baggage of presuppositions with us. According to these we frame the text or choose our lens. Without this we would flail about in a sea of misunderstanding. We would be unable to interpret. The process is similar to that of a conversation. We interact with the other, we interact with the text. The meaning is created in that interaction. But once we have used our particular interpretative key, the text is still ultimately 'other'. It is precisely that 'otherness' which makes it a classic. This 'otherness' is not to be confused with a 'once and for all essence' to be distilled from the text. The text is not a container into which meaning, divine or otherwise, was poured centuries before and which is waiting to be drawn out by the contemporary, ever more sophisticated exegete. The 'otherness' of the text lies in its ability to claim our attention now, in this time, in this place, to continue to speak a living word. The question I ask is, 'To what does this text invite us now?' Thus the meaning of any text of scripture, which is a classic in a very particular sense — a text by which a community claims to live — is not only susceptible to change in each generation but indeed must change as the culture and circumstances change. To take one extreme example, the story from the Hebrew Scriptures of the sacrifice of Isaac and the testing of the faith of Abraham must now be read in the shadow of the Holocaust with its countless 'burnt offerings'.[5] The context alters the text. Liberation theologians discovered this when familiar texts read from the perspective of the poor became radically different — became radical. In a similar way reading from a feminist perspective has altered not only the interpreters but also the texts themselves. For me this has been one of the most fascinating aspects of this whole endeavour: watching how familiar texts oddly comforting, if slightly boring, have shaped themselves so differently as I have attempted to read them 'against the grain'. They have compelled my attention again.

I make no pretence of reading as a dispassionate observer — I am not. I read with an urgency asking whether these familiar texts can be life-giving for women and men today. Can these dry bones live? Can they be claimed by women, in particular, as part of their tradition? Can women be nourished for their faith journey from these roots? And can they be proclaimed for the whole Christian community as 'the word of God'? It is not immediately obvious that the answer to these questions is in the affirmative. It is all too easy to demonstrate the androcentric, patriarchal and sexist structure of scriptural texts and to illustrate the same imbalance on the side of interpretations of those texts. It is not surprising that many women have simply washed their hands of that tradition and gone to other wells. However there remains a considerable body of women for whom this is not an option and who, in the words of Phyllis Trible, insist on staying and struggling with the text, refusing to let go 'without a blessing'.[6] Scripture scholar Sandra Schneiders describes scripture as 'witness to revelation' and uses the hermeneutical method of interpretation outlined above: 'Meaning is not contained in the text; it is an event of understanding which takes place in the encounter between text and reader.'[7] She goes on to argue that the Christian community is not the passive recipient of revelation but the active subject so she too argues for an engagement with the text, a dialectical process which may result in some texts being judged as seriously flawed, which will recognise that certain texts are descriptive rather than prescriptive, and which will seek to discern how the community can continue to bear witness to the Word.

These approaches are at quite a remove from any simplistic notion of 'Women in the Bible' as constituting the principal feminist concern. In the early stages of feminist scholarship generated by the awareness of the absence of women from scripture and tradition there was a tendency to highlight stories about women. The problem with this approach was that it tended to perpetuate the notion of women as 'others' to the far more numerous men, whose experience remained normative. Increasingly feminist perspectives — and they vary greatly — tend to concern themselves with the whole of scripture. So even when the primary — although not exclusive — concern is with texts in which women feature, as in the case of these essays, there is a much wider dimension at work in the process.

For example, I have chosen to look at the 'place of women' within certain texts and then the 'place' of those texts in the wider context in order to explore the ways in which stories about women are treated, both within the gospels and by those interpreting them. In doing this I hope to highlight the significance of gender in the story and in the reader. I read these texts from the perspective of a Christian feminist concerned with the restrictions and the possibilities for the discipleship and ministry of contemporary women. My methodology is to read these texts against the grain, and my concern is to discover what energy there might be in these texts for the transformation of the Christian community today. As I have already indicated, this is a committed stance, but whilst it does not seek to impose itself, it desires instead to invite others to see with a different eye. Seeing differently seems to me to be one of the central joys and delights of this enterprise, a joy of which I was again reminded when I listened to A. S. Byatt turning the precious stone, which is Luke's story of Mary and Martha, to a different light. It should not be a case of 'the feminist perspective' as a reverse dominance, a new orthodoxy, but rather about feminist strands weaving or connecting their stories to the stories of the community of interpreters who seek to keep the tradition alive by continuous conversation with its texts. Ultimately the adequacy or inadequacy of the interpretations will be judged not by the scholars alone but primarily by those who live by the consequences. A telling illustration of this truth is found in the reception of biblical texts among African-American slaves. On the one hand the Bible was used to legitimise slavery, but that same Bible became for many their primary source of liberation, enabling them to resist and refuse the injunctions about slavery: 'I promised my Maker that if I ever learned to read and if freedom came, I would not read that part of the Bible.'[8] The 'canon within the canon' for many feminist and liberation theologians is the prophetic principle of liberation for all peoples. So scripture itself, as well as interpretations of scripture, can be used against scripture. Thus in the example above the message proclaimed by Jesus in the synagogue at Nazareth, 'to let the oppressed go free' — which resonates with and echoes the prophets — stands as a sharp judgment against the culturally conditioned texts from Paul about the place of women or slaves.

In my essays I use this criterion, for example, in my own reading of the story of Mary and Martha from Luke to which I have given the deliberately ambiguous title, 'Serving Women'. My intention is to resist the idea of the appropriate role of woman as servant and to ask whose interests are served by the story. Does the story as traditionally told serve the interests of women? In what ways, if any, can it serve as a liberating text for women?

This forms part of the process of subverting the text. The story of the Canaanite woman, as told by Matthew, or the Syro-Phoenician woman, as told by Mark, in itself can be seen as an illustration of this process of subversion at work. The woman, according to the narrator in Matthew's Gospel, takes the comment of Jesus, 'It is not fair to take the children's food and throw it to the dogs', and subverts it: 'Even the dogs eat the crumbs which fall from the master's table.' (Matt. 15: 26, 27) The woman takes the image and turns it, recasting it in her favour, and in the process converts Jesus himself!

A further stage in this process is what I describe as 'removing the brackets'. It seems to me that stories about women have tended to be privatised and domesticated, read as self-contained moral tales. Once again we can call on the familiar Martha and Mary story to serve as an example. This text has generally been read as a domestic dispute between two women which is then psychoanalysed into an unhappy dualism between the contemplative and active life. Commentators remind their readers, for example, that 'housework is not the demand of the moment'. Indeed it is not! If we release this little tale from its domestic brackets it flows out as a text about discipleship and practices of ministry.

The lens of gender in itself is raised as an issue in dealing with texts which look beyond gender. This is done to illustrate the complex interconnection of gender with race and class and culture. It is not enough simply to highlight women's experience without asking, which women? Whose experience? This issue is illustrated by an essay on a less familiar text, that of Lydia in Acts 16. Contained in the story of the conversion of Lydia is another tale, the story of a slave girl. Telling her story becomes a metaphor which challenges any simplistic view of 'Women in Scripture' and reminds us again of the primacy of the canon of liberation for all people, and particularly for the most oppressed.

Reading against the grain has not always meant reading from the perspective of the female character. Sometimes it has involved de-centring that character in order to appreciate a different dynamic in the story. For example in Luke's story entitled in the NRSV (New Revised Standard Version) 'A Sinful Woman Forgiven' the interests of the woman are not served by focusing on her sinfulness but on her function in exposing Jesus as the prophet. We do this by shifting the attention away from her and towards Simon, who after all is the one principally in need of enlightenment. In a similar way interpretations of the classic text, The Prodigal Son, are blocked, precisely by that title. Stripping the younger son of his central place allows for a much more interesting dynamic to emerge. Of course this story also challenges us by its total absence of female characters: 'The tale of the absent mother and missing sisters!'

On the whole I have chosen familiar texts and — apart from one text from Luke-Acts — all the others are from the synoptic Gospels. Although John's Gospel provides a rich resource of stories concerning women and an interesting context for a feminist perspective, the genre is so different that I felt it would be better served by a separate treatment.

I start with those stories where women are usually the focus of the text and explore them in terms of gender and of context — marking their place in the flow of the gospel. Then I move to less well-known stories where women feature by their absence, rather than by their presence, or where the focus of the text is elsewhere. These sections are not watertight and some texts fit both categories.

Each text is treated as a separate entity, but readers may find common themes and images which resonate and echo as they move from one to the other. Hopefully these will swell to a conviction that conversations such as the ones started in these pages need to be taken out into the places where people gather as church. I have given each chapter a heading which refers to women even where only one woman is mentioned in the story. My intention here is to connect the place of women within these stories with the place of women in the churches today.

This brings me to my final point. If the ultimate concern in conversing with these texts is transformation — personal and communal — then one important stage on that journey is proclamation. Although it is possible to hear women preaching in many of the Christian churches, this happens by exception only, by permission and not according to charism or gift, in the Roman Catholic tradition. It is regrettable, to say the least, that this office is still linked with the orders which exclude women and indeed most men. This seems to me to be one of the ministries which when extended to women, will have enormous repercussions. The breaking of that dam of silence among Roman Catholic women will have a powerful cathartic effect — if the experience of the Anglican and indeed Jewish women is anything to go by[9] — and it will be a grace for the whole Church. However we need not merely to hear women breaking the word on a regular basis, but we also need a feminist perspective on preaching. Part of that perspective will involve reading scripture against the grain so that the voices from the margins both within the text and the assembly may be heard. My hope is that this 'baker's dozen' of essays will set some dough rising to that effect!

PLACING WOMEN

Gender and Text Set in Context

Chapter 1

Visiting Women

In those days Mary set out and went with haste to a Judean town in the hill country, where she entered the house of Zechariah and greeted Elizabeth. When Elizabeth heard Mary's greeting, the child leaped in her womb. And Elizabeth was filled with the Holy Spirit and exclaimed with a loud cry, 'Blessed are you among women and blessed is the fruit of your womb. And why has this happened to me that the mother of my Lord comes to me? For as soon as I heard the sound of your greeting, the child in my womb leaped for joy. And blessed is she who believed that there would be a fulfilment of what was spoken to her by the Lord.' And Mary said, 'My soul magnifies the Lord, and my spirit rejoices in God my saviour, for he has looked with favour on the lowliness of his servant. Surely from now on all generations will call me blessed; for the Mighty One has done great things for me and holy is his name. His mercy is on those who fear him from generation to generation. He has shown strength with his arm; he has scattered the proud in the thoughts of their hearts. He has brought down the powerful from their thrones, and lifted up the lowly; he has filled the hungry with good things, and sent the rich away empty. He has helped his servant Israel, in remembrance of his mercy, according to the promise he made to our ancestors, to Abraham and to his descendants forever.'
And Mary remained with her about three months and returned to her home.(Luke 1: 39–56)

Having chosen to read these texts from the perspective of gender, there is a delight in beginning with that rare event — a story about two women! Even more unusual is the fact that these women, unlike many other pairs of women in the Hebrew Scriptures,[1] and unlike the pair we look at in the next chapter, Martha and Mary, are not rivals. However, before we get completely carried away, it is well to recognise one biblical convention which is not challenged: they will both rejoice in the births of sons. The time of daughters has not yet come. Yet before those births our text celebrates a sacred time of solidarity between these two women and their shared experiences. For a very brief interlude in this gospel we have a 'women's room'. The visitation is a perfect example of a text so familiar that, paradoxically, we may fail to see it. On one level it is such a simple short story: Mary comes to visit Elizabeth, stays for a while and goes home again. What happens? They talk! It is a perfect 'short story', not a drama, there is no action — just conversation taking place within the limited setting of the visit. Mary arrives, greetings are exchanged, a dialogue ensues, she stays with her cousin about three months and then returns home. The conversation reported to us takes place in the first moments of their encounter and then the doors close over and we remain outside. Yet in that short time when we as listeners or readers are drawn in to eavesdrop in the house of Zechariah, something of great importance occurs. From our perspective looking at the place of women we can observe two women displaced by untimely pregnancies seeking to interpret their experiences, seeking to know their place.

From the perspective of the narrator the visitation episode connects the two separate stories of the annunciation of the births of John the Baptist and of Jesus. It is a point of intersection in the longer story which started in the temple with Zechariah and will conclude with the birth of John. This story of John becomes in turn the prologue to the story of the birth of Jesus. No further incident is reported but the events which have occurred are taken up and interpreted.

In between the annunciation to Zechariah and the births of the promised sons we have an encounter between two women which creates the context for the proclamation of the Magnificat. I want to focus on this meeting and go back and forth from this place, a Judean town in the hill country, to look at what has gone before and what is still to come. The perspective from which we will read the annunciation accounts and the births will be that of these women. For a very brief interlude in a story with two male heroes, 'He will be great in the sight of the Lord' (1: 14) and 'He will be great and will be called the Son of the most High' (1: 32), we find ourselves in the women's space.

The house may be described as 'the house of Zechariah' but as a consequence of his failure to trust in the message of the angel, Zechariah has been struck dumb and so the only words which are heard are those of Mary and Elizabeth. The house of Zechariah has become for these months a house of women.

We have become so accustomed to the familiar lines which introduce the annunciation story, 'And in the sixth month', we may forget the point of reference. This is the first instance of the shift in perspective. The story has changed from Zechariah's story to that of Elizabeth. The narrative no longer speaks of the days or months of Herod's reign, or Zechariah's service, but refers now to the sixth month of Elizabeth's pregnancy. Elizabeth has now been brought into focus just as Zechariah fades from sight as well as hearing. At the end of the scene in the temple Zechariah comes out to the people who are waiting for a blessing. 'He kept motioning to them and remained unable to speak. When his time of service was ended, he went to his home.' (1: 23)

Immediately the focus turns to Elizabeth. 'After those days his wife Elizabeth conceived, and for five months she remained in seclusion.' (1: 24) Not without considerable irony do we note that it is only when Zechariah has been silenced that we hear Elizabeth speak! Neither angelic messenger nor husband nor even the narrator speaks for her. She interprets her own experience: 'This is what the Lord has done for me when he looked favourably on me and took away the disgrace I have endured among my people.' (1: 25) Earlier the narrator has told us that both Zechariah and Elizabeth 'were righteous before God' but childless because Elizabeth was barren. Now Elizabeth understands this pregnancy as a blessing for her. Her shame has been taken away. The angel had promised a son to Zechariah but for Elizabeth this is something 'the Lord has done for me'. Zechariah had doubted the power of God and so was rendered mute; Elizabeth rejoices in God's blessing and is given voice to express it. She is the first person in this Gospel who receives 'the good news for the poor'. It should not surprise us then that the time-scale is shifted from the chronology of rulers and priests to that of this pregnant and prophetic woman. Just as in his turn her son will prepare the way of the Lord, Elizabeth is the first to do so. It is a mark of how blind our reading has been that commentators have failed to appreciate the prophetic role of Elizabeth. The emphasis has been on the annunciation to Zechariah and his subsequent silencing and the placing of John among the prophetic figures of Israel. Elizabeth is not recognised as belonging to the line of prophets. Her gender excludes her. So when we read the story from her perspective we are startled to hear her speak and to realise that she too has a history, that she too has her place among the faithful women and men whose trust is rewarded and who recognise what has happened and who has come to her. Elizabeth's seclusion lasts five months and is broken by her own commentary on her situation. The seclusion of Zechariah will not be broken until he confirms the words of Elizabeth, 'His name is John.' (1: 63) For the duration of the pregnancy and until the naming of John it is Elizabeth who speaks, who initiates, who leads. It is by the lunar time-scale of her pregnancy that we are guided: 'for five months' (1: 24), 'In the sixth month' (1: 26), 'this is the sixth month' (1: 36), 'about three months' (1: 56), until 'And now the time came for Elizabeth to give birth.' (1: 57) So despite the patriarchal framing of the birth stories of John, 'In the days of King Herod of Judea, there was a priest named Zechariah . . .' (Luke 1: 5) and then of Jesus, 'In those days a decree went out from Emperor Augustus . . .' (Luke 2: 1), there is a shift, a period of ten lunar months, where this time-scale is suspended and where we mark time by Elizabeth's pregnancy.[2]

It is Elizabeth's accurate reading of her own experience which enables her to understand the meaning of her cousin's pregnancy. There is an extraordinary, explosive moment of insight when the two women greet one another: 'When Elizabeth heard Mary's greeting, the child leaped in her womb. And Elizabeth was filled with the Holy Spirit and exclaimed with a loud cry, "Blessed are you among women and blessed is the fruit of your womb."' There can be no clearer indication of Elizabeth as prophet than this. She is described as 'filled with the Holy Spirit', the same Spirit with which her child will be filled, the same Spirit which has come upon Mary, the same Spirit which will fill Jesus. She cries out with a loud voice. Her loud cry signals her prophecy. It is with a loud cry that Jesus gives up his Spirit at his death. It is with a loud cry that Elizabeth recognises his conception. This woman, whose husband has been struck dumb, unable to give the blessing, blesses Mary and blesses the child of her womb. Later Zechariah is described as 'filled with the Holy Spirit' and '[he] spoke this prophecy' (1: 67). But the first prophetic voice to be heard in Luke's Gospel is that of Elizabeth, 'Blessed are you among women and blessed is the fruit of your womb.' (1: 42) She greets Mary first in her own right, 'Blessed are you among women', and then she acknowledges 'the fruit of the womb'. She concludes her greeting with praise of Mary's faith, 'And blessed is she who believed . . .' Mary the faithful disciple takes precedence over Mary the mother, a point confirmed later in the Gospel when Jesus responds to the acclamation, 'Blessed is the womb that bore you', with 'Blessed rather are those who hear the word of God and obey it!' (11: 27–28) The prophetic expression does not conclude with the blessing but continues with Elizabeth's recognition of Mary as 'the mother of my Lord'. Elizabeth is the first to name the child as 'Lord'. We notice too that just as Elizabeth had recognised the grace of the pregnancy as something the Lord has done for her, so here too she asks, 'Why has this happened to me, that the mother of my Lord comes to me?' There is nothing abstract or theoretical about the workings of the Spirit in this episode. Through Elizabeth's words we see how grace is mediated as the women become a source of blessing for one another. The description of the child 'leaping in the womb' is the first sign of this incarnational grace. One might be mistaken about angelic visitors but there is no mistaking the kicking of the child in the womb! Elizabeth's greeting enfolds Mary and gathers her into the space she has cleared with her understanding and rejoicing in her own pregnancy, a space where God is named as the one who looks favourably on the poor, who takes away both the shame of the barren woman and the shame of the vulnerable pregnant girl. Although the meeting of the two pregnant women has traditionally been described as one of great joy, indeed as 'a collision of joys', I think this is premature until the singing out of the Magnificat. Elizabeth's pregnancy has taken away her shame but, as Matthew makes very clear in his reading of the situation, Mary's pregnancy could well be the source of 'disgrace among the people' (Matt. 1: 19). Although Luke does not emphasise that interpretation, the Magnificat makes little sense if one does not read it as a transformation of the situation of both women. Mary goes 'with haste' to Elizabeth less to offer support, or to share the 'good news' of the pregnancy, a conventional reading, than to verify what has happened, to learn about the God who has 'visited them' in extraordinarily ordinary ways. Elizabeth's greeting makes it clear that what has occurred should be named as a blessing, 'Blessed are you among women, and blessed is the fruit of your womb.'

Fear gives way to joy and Mary utters her song of praise. Some manuscripts attribute the Magnificat to Elizabeth, but even if we accept the majority consensus and read it as Mary's utterance, it is Elizabeth who has prepared the way for that canticle. The elder pregnant woman becomes midwife to the Word. She hears Mary into speech. There is nothing tentative about this conversation, it is powerful and empowering. In fact it should be possible to hear the Magnificat as a song for two voices as it picks up echoes from both the stories and as it resonates with the songs of the biblical women.

The opening line connects this Miriam of Nazareth with Miriam, sister of Moses, who sang to the people, 'Sing to the Lord for he has triumphed gloriously.' (Exod. 15: 21) It also links the once barren Elizabeth with the once barren Hannah, 'My heart exults in the Lord . . . He raises up the poor from the dust; he lifts the needy from the ash heap.' (1 Sam. 2: 1–10) The pregnancies are seen as symbols of God's compassion for the poor, a compassion made flesh in the wombs of women. Some scholars have pointed out the semantic connection between the words for 'compassion' and for 'womb' having the same Hebrew root. It seems to be helpful and appropriate to think of the Magnificat as a song of solidarity from both women as this is the only time we have a scriptural account of two pregnant women who are not described as rivals. For the other pairs of women, Sarah and Hagar (Gen. 16; 21), Hannah and Peninnah (1 Sam. 1), a source of joy for one becomes a source of pain for the other. 'When she saw she had conceived she looked with contempt upon her mistress.' (Gen. 16: 4) The God who is celebrated is also a partisan God, 'the barren has borne seven but she who has many children is forlorn'.

In contrast, Mary and Elizabeth together usher in a new era where disputes about 'which one of them is to be regarded as the greatest' are replaced with the model of the 'one who serves' (Luke 22: 27). This is anticipated in the hospitality of Elizabeth to Mary, where Mary is welcomed not as a threat to the well-being of Elizabeth and her child but rather as grace and blessing.

The Magnificat serves to turn the attention of the story from the visit of one woman to another to the shared recognition of both women that God has visited them. It is God's visitation which is the primary focus, 'My soul magnifies the Lord and my spirit rejoices in God my saviour . . . He has filled the hungry with good things . . .' The prophetic words of Mary of Nazareth prepare the way for the proclamation in the synagogue in Nazareth, 'The Spirit of the Lord is upon me, because he has anointed me to bring good news to the poor.' (Luke 4: 18) This is the first instance of that message which is quite literally embodied in these women. The Word has taken flesh in them. When we recognise the primary focus of the story, then we understand how to read around the periphery. It is not the virginity of Mary or the barrenness of Elizabeth in themselves which concern the narrator, but the need to demonstrate that 'nothing is impossible with God' and that this is a God who has 'lifted up the lowly'.

Mary is not 'blessed among women' because she is virgin and

with child but because she is hospitable to God's visitation. Divine paternity is not the issue but divine agency and, even more important, right relationship to God is, 'The Mighty one has done great things for me and Holy is his name.' (1: 49)

Both Mary and Elizabeth stress the 'for me', yet in both cases the apparently private revelation sends out ripples which move it from the particular to the universal. The 'for me' in the first verses of the Magnificat quickly becomes a mercy which extends 'from generation to generation'. In Elizabeth's case this is illustrated by the spreading of the news of the birth and the naming of John 'throughout the entire hill country of Judea' (1: 65).

Right relationship makes it possible for these women to respond positively and to speak prophetically. They are witnesses to the Word, they are bearers of the Word. In fact we could best describe them as 'good gossips'. Writer and theologian Sara Maitland drew my attention to the original meaning of a word now used in an almost exclusively sexist and derogatory manner.[3] 'The idle tittle-tattle', usually of women about trifling matters, is the current definition but in original usage the word meant variously 'a sponsor at baptism' or 'a woman friend who comes to attend a birth' or 'one who is *sib in God*, that is, spiritually related'. I was stunned when I first read these definitions and checked them in the dictionary, saddened to see 'archaic' in brackets beside the earlier meanings. It seemed such an extraordinary path for a word to travel from sacred and holy in meaning to become trivialised and denigrated. In some ways it seemed a powerful symbol for the denigration of the experience of women. Elizabeth and Mary, powerful prophets of the Word, did not become the foremothers of women as prophets and preachers of the Word but of women as passive and submissive 'handmaidens'. We need to retrieve the goodness of 'gossip' and the power and potential of women's naming of religious experience. 'The Visitation' is not primarily a pious text or a beautiful tale about two women thanking God for their pregnancies, however important that may be, but a subversive story of women's solidarity in their suffering, of women's power in their prophecy, of women's recognition of the 'visitation of

God' who brings down the powerful and lifts up the lowly. In bringing Mary and Elizabeth together to proclaim this good news the narrator connects the old Israel and the new, establishing both continuity and discontinuity. The door of the temple and the mouth of Zechariah are closed up and the wombs of women become the holy places of revelation. The gospel of liberation is sung out from the mouths of women just as at the end of Luke the good news of the resurrection is heard from the lips of women. The line of continuity in faithful witness needs to be redrawn connecting Elizabeth and Mary to women like Miriam and Hannah who have preceded them, and to Mary Magdalene and the other witnesses of the resurrection who follow them, and down through the ages picking up the threads of the histories of women who have heard and proclaimed the Word 'from generation to generation'.

In the end the doors close over once more and the patriarchal framing and naming once again eclipse the stories of the women. Zechariah's mouth is opened and, confirming Elizabeth's naming of the child, he pours forth his own canticle of praise. We do not hear from Elizabeth again. The time-scale reverts to that marked by the reigns of emperors and governors, Augustus and Quirinius, and after the birth and the presentation of the child Jesus we hear no response from Mary other than that 'she pondered these things in her heart'. Simeon speaks, but the words of the 'prophet' Anna are not directly reported. The women have been silenced.

Each time we revisit this text the silence is broken and the voices of Mary and Elizabeth are heard again as women singing out hope.

CHAPTER 2

SERVING WOMEN

Now as they went on their way, he entered a certain village, where a woman named Martha welcomed him into her home. She had a sister named Mary, who sat at the Lord's feet and listened to what he was saying. But Martha was distracted by her many tasks; so she came to him and asked, 'Lord, do you not care that my sister has left me to do all the work by myself? Tell her then to help me.' But the Lord answered her, 'Martha, Martha, you are worried and distracted by many things; there is need of only one thing. Mary has chosen the better part, which will not be taken away from her.' (Luke 10: 38–42)

O what a difficult text! Each time I announce to a particular women's group that I want to work with this story, a collective sigh goes up around the room. Yet again and again I choose the text as an excellent illustration of the challenges facing women when they read the Scriptures. I have chosen a deliberately ambiguous title to illustrate the ambiguities of the text. This is a piece about women serving, but does it serve women?

The problem for women is clear: the story pits two women against one another and not alone is there an absence of female solidarity but this is apparently endorsed by Jesus. The women gathering to discuss the text are very often women who do indeed spend much of their lives 'busy with many things' and would truly love the opportunity to take some time out for themselves but cannot easily do so. This story makes them feel both angry and guilty. They feel angry that Martha's role is not given support and that her work goes unrecognised and unpraised. It makes women feel guilty that they do not have the time for their 'spiritual' lives. It forces a choice between the two women portrayed or involves a complex psychological exercise whereby women speak of the dualism within themselves: the external Martha and the internal Mary. It reinforces a spiritual/material dualism. Traditional rendering of the story has narrowed our vision of it so that we see a dichotomy between the supposedly mundane tasks of Martha and the superior contemplative role of Mary. That Mary has chosen the better part becomes the rationale for the superiority of a religious vocation over that of the married state. Whatever way we read the story it leaves us at least uncomfortable and probably angry and resentful. But this is anger which until relatively recently has not been given expression. Women have, like Mary, listened; now, like Martha, they are talking back!

The story has been read to women by men, it has been preached to women by a male-only clergy, it has been one of many texts used consciously or unconsciously to reinforce particular gender stereotypes. The quiet, docile, passive Mary is praised; the complaining, noisy — or from a different perspective — the assertive Martha is reprimanded.

When we work with this text the first task is to demythologise it to free it from the pious trappings which have rendered it anaemic and to give Martha and Mary a voice. I ask the women to read and respond to the story as a story and not primarily as a piece of inspired or sacred scripture, to remove the blocks which might inhibit an honest response. I suggest that we should read against the grain of the text. Read it with resistance. Refuse the pull towards the dominant narrator's voice and allow other voices to emerge. Then when we have grappled with our own responses I ask the groups to divide into Martha and Mary groups and read the story again from the particular perspective of one or other of these women. 'I am Martha' is a powerful point of entry into the story. It is interesting that the groups designated as Marthas are considerably more enthusiastic than the groups named as Marys. Through Martha, years of resentment and anger felt by many women can be released. There is an injustice to be addressed here and Martha's protests are vociferous. Hearing Martha speak is a liberating experience. The woman put down by Luke's narrative rises to challenge the interpretations of her role. 'You'd have something else to complain about if there was no dinner on the table!' 'If it was a man serving you, you'd have praised him to the skies; but a woman, you take it for granted and then you criticise her!' 'When men serve it is called "ministry"; when women serve it is women serving!' 'They are even expected to get up out of their sick-beds and serve, like Peter's mother-in-law.'

Mary, although more reluctant to speak — it is after all more difficult to challenge praise than criticism — eventually finds her voice. This is one of the interesting insights: the recognition that Mary has not been given a voice in the text. Mary, apparently praised for conforming to a patriarchal expectation of female docility, speaks. Yes, it was a relief to be given the freedom to choose a different role. Yes, she welcomed being invited to sit and listen for a change. This was a liberating moment for her and the invitation was there for Martha also; but Martha had not seen it, she had refused the possibility of moving outside her role. It was Martha, not Mary, who was conforming! Mary was not passive, she chose this part. It was about choice.

The conversation flows and the voices engage in dialogue continually opening new ways of hearing the story. Anger is expressed, energy and, always, laughter is released and the story engages us all at many different levels. It ceases to be oppressive and paradoxically becomes a means of liberation as women tell it differently. The story connected with the lives of women and their experience starts to shape itself differently.

Listening to the conversations I realise just how powerful social conditioning can be. We read this text domestically, we interpret it within that sphere. Texts about women are texts about women. They are not read as texts which concern all human beings. So this story has been told essentially as a minor moral tale. It suggests, according to received wisdom, that domestic concerns must take second place to attending to the Word of God. The context is a woman's space, the kitchen; the content concerns an argument between women about women's work. It appears to be rather trivial, particularly in comparison with the parable about the Good Samaritan, which precedes the story of Mary and Martha in Luke's gospel and has the merit of considerable more dramatic action to illustrate its moral!

This story tends to be treated, again like many concerns of women, as if it were placed in brackets. It is very rare indeed in commentaries to see it linked up with preceding or following texts in the Gospel. It is as if stories about women belonged to a separate genre. There is a temptation in feminist readings to perpetuate this notion. Feminist interpretation must ultimately concern itself with the whole canon and not just with passages about women.[1]

In what turned out to be a perfect illustration of how gender marks our reading of such texts, I tried an experiment with one group. I took this story and read it aloud a second time to a group after they had spent considerable time working on it. I made one small change, one small alteration, and the same story was greeted with a stunned silence. 'Now as they went on their way, he entered a certain village where a man named James welcomed him into his house. . . . John sat at the Lord's feet and listened to what he was saying. . . . "My brother has left me to do the serving . . ."'

There was a palpable shock as we all recognised just how influenced we were by the gender of the characters. This seemed to be a different story. We were listening to a story about roles and ministries and discipleship. The story had slipped its domestic confines and moved into the public sphere simply by virtue of the fact that the characters were male and therefore presumed to have a public role.

Alert to the new possibilities we heard the text again. We removed the brackets and read the story in the flow of the Lucan text. 'Now as they were on their way . . .' In Luke's Gospel 'the way' is significant. Jesus is on a journey, his face is set towards Jerusalem. As he goes he instructs his disciples; they learn as they journey. Nowhere is that more vividly depicted than on the road to Emmaus — but here too journeying and teaching belong together. This story is a journey story. We can link it back to the beginning of the chapter where the disciples are sent ahead in pairs 'to every town and place where he himself intended to go'(10: 1). The disciples have been sent out in pairs and now we read that Jesus enters a house of a pair who, by their welcome,

indicate that they are disciples. Martha's welcome is like that of
Zaccheus (19: 6), it is the fulsome welcome of one who is open
to the prophet. It is significant too that Martha does the
welcoming. She appears to be a woman of status. It is she who
is the householder. Like Lydia in Acts 16, or Joanna or Susanna
in Luke 8: 3, she is able to provide, to offer hospitality to the
disciples. It therefore seems inappropriate to interpret 'the many
tasks' so literally — Martha with red face and hands dusty with
flour, begging Mary to give her a hand with the washing up! We
can presume, I think, that this is a full household, including
servants. The naming of two characters does not exclude the
presence of many other unnamed members of the household.
Again I suggest that if 'James' were the named householder and
host we would make such an assumption. So if Martha is not
protesting about the absence of domestic assistance what is the
point of her enquiry?

The NRSV refers to Martha's 'many tasks', and this is a
translation of the Greek word *diakonia* — more accurately
translated as 'serving'. The same word is used by Jesus at the
Passover meal when a dispute about authority arises among the
disciples and Jesus reminds them that he is among them as one
who serves (22: 27). In Acts 6: 1–4 there is a discussion about
the ministry of the table and the ministry of the Word. The same
word is used. This results in the appointment of seven deacons
to help with the task! So what happens if we release this story
from its domestic confines. It shifts its perspective and becomes
a story about ministry and the roles of the disciples. If we see it
as a parallel text to the one in Acts then it could well be read as
a story concerning an area which caused some dispute in the
Lucan Church. We know from Paul's letters that women were
appointed as deacons. Is the reprimand to Martha an indication
that women were indeed exercising roles of leadership within the
Lucan community? Is this an attempt to restrict or open out
such roles? It could be read either way. It may be an attempt to
discredit the ministry of women as some commentators have
argued.[2] On the other hand I would argue that the text testifies
to the existence of the ministry of women exercised through

house churches, of which this clearly is one. Is the affirmation of Mary's role important because of the emphasis on the Word? Perhaps the ministry of women was restricted to particular tasks; perhaps this opens out rather than closes down possibilities. Women are not confined to the ministry of the table — if that is the implication — but may also be involved in the ministry of the Word. Mary is welcomed as a disciple. To sit at the feet of the master is not an act of female submission but the appropriate position for a disciple. These are all possible readings. The text opens up to various readings which have implications in a wider ecclesiological context, so it should not be privatised as spiritual direction or moral instruction or trivialised as a domestic conflict.

Gender affects our reading on many levels. When, for example, disputes arise between male disciples, as for example between the named James and John in the Gospels of Mark (10: 35–44) and Matthew (20: 20–28), or between the unnamed disciples in Luke (22: 24), these are generally interpreted as creative forms of conflict opening to greater insight. They are not read as a dismissal of the ministry of men in general! Martha and Mary likewise represent discipleship and we must ask what the important issues are here and, of course, ultimately we want to know if this text has any relevance to our lives as contemporary church women.

Even when we extend this text into a wider sphere and paint it on to the broader canvas of Church and ministry, the ambiguities do not disappear. Why is *diakonia*, upheld as the model for ministry by Jesus, not supported here? The tensions cannot and perhaps should not be glossed over. In this instance, as in many others, women as readers of sacred scripture have to learn to negotiate their way through dangerous territory in their search for a living, life-giving word.

One tentative solution, which is only partial, may be to recognise that the difference in gender roles may demand a different assessment of models of ministry for men and women. The radical self-description of Jesus as 'one who serves' receives its shocking power because of the very strong role reversal. Jesus waiting at table, Jesus washing the feet of the disciples, was performing tasks regularly or traditionally carried out by female slaves. Women carrying out such tasks were seen then as they are now as women fulfilling their expected roles. Women have traditionally been socialised into caring roles and fulfil these whether they are paid poorly or not at all. Such roles when assumed by men become professions. In that light the invitation to Mary to sit and listen, which is a precondition for eventually becoming a teacher or rabbi oneself, is liberating and empowering for her. We are still left with the difficulty of the apparent downgrading of the ministry of Martha. We cannot smooth out this tension, nor should we, but we can continue to question the text and question the restrictions which are put on women who attempt to exercise ministry in the contemporary Church. We can refuse the divisions in the text, we can resist the denial of the ministry of Martha, but it can alert us to the problems of women assuming too many tasks which are taken for granted, taken as naturally gendered and not affirmed as ministries.

So does this story of serving women actually serve the interests of women? The answer can, I think, be a modified 'yes'. It serves the interests of women who are willing to engage with the text, to wrestle with it until finally, although wounded, we can limp away with a blessing.[3] The blessing here may be holy rage or it may be greater insight as we recognise that women from the earliest times questioned and explored their role in the Christian community. We can at least continue the practice.

Chapter 3

Suffering Women

When Jesus had crossed again in a boat to the other side, a great crowd gathered around him; and he was by the sea. Then one of the leaders of the synagogue named Jairus came and when he saw him, fell at his feet and begged him repeatedly, 'My little daughter is at the point of death. Come and lay your hands on her, that she may be made well, and live.' So he went with him. And a large crowd followed him and pressed in on him. Now there was a woman who had been suffering from haemorrhages for twelve years. She had endured much under many physicians, and had spent all she had; and she was no better, but rather grew worse.

She had heard about Jesus, and came up behind him in the crowd and touched his cloak, for she said, 'If I but touch his clothes I will be made well.' Immediately her haemorrhage stopped; and she felt in her body that she was healed of the disease. Immediately aware that power had gone forth from him, Jesus turned about in the crowd and said, 'Who touched my clothes?' And his disciples said to him, 'You can see the crowd pressing in on you; how can you say, "Who touched me?"' He looked all around to see who had done it. But the woman knowing what had happened to her came in fear and trembling, fell down before him and told him the whole truth. He said to her, 'Daughter, your faith has made you well; go in peace, and be healed of your disease.'

While he was still speaking, some people came from the leader's house to say, 'Your daughter is dead. Why trouble the teacher any further?' But overhearing what they said, Jesus said to the leader of the synagogue, 'Do not fear, only believe.' He allowed no one to follow him except Peter, James, and John, the brother of James. When they came to the house of the leader of the synagogue, he saw a commotion, people weeping and wailing loudly. When he had entered, he said to them, 'Why do you make such a commotion and weep? The child is not dead but

sleeping.' And they all laughed at him. Then he put them all
outside, and took the child's father and mother and those who
were with him and went in where the child was.
He took her by the hand and said to her, 'Talitha cum', which
means, 'Little girl, get up!' And immediately the girl got up and
began to walk about [she was twelve years of age]. At this they
were overcome with amazement. He strictly ordered them that
no one should know about this, and told them to give her
something to eat. (Mark 5: 21–43)

This story of the two healings is also told in the Gospels of
Matthew and Luke but Mark's version is the most detailed.
From the perspective of the women within the story and from
the perspective of women readers it is the most interesting.

We notice first that the story of the woman with the
haemorrhage is framed by the story of the daughter of Jairus.
This intersecting of the two healings makes it not only possible
but inevitable that they form a commentary on one another. For
Matthew, the story of the woman appears incidental: it is not
intrinsically connected with the healing of the official's daughter.
Both Mark and Luke, on the other hand, use the number twelve
to link their female characters and in fact to draw them into the
most intimate of relationships: one is on the threshold of
menstruation; the other has not ceased to bleed for twelve years.

The juxtaposition of the stories allows us to make further
contrasts. We have two suppliants, one male, one female. The first
male figure is not only named as Jairus but has a position in the
community. He is described as a leader of the synagogue. The
daughter, on whose behalf he pleads, receives her status through
her relationship with her father. The woman, on the other hand,
is unnamed. She is not even described by her relationship to a
male, let alone by any place in society, but instead by her suffering,
suffering which disqualifies her from any position. She is regarded
as ritually unclean according to the regulations of Leviticus:

If a woman has a discharge of blood for many days, not at the
time of her impurity, or if she has a discharge beyond the time

of her impurity, all the days of the discharge she shall continue in uncleanness; as in the days of her impurity she shall be unclean. Every bed on which she lies . . . shall be treated as the bed of her impurity; and everything on which she sits shall be unclean . . . Whoever touches these things shall be unclean. (Lev. 15: 25–7)

The contrast could hardly be stronger between the respected male figure and the disgraced female, between one honoured by society and one who is shunned and cast out. Her chronic condition renders her a social leper.

The supplication of Jairus is a very public one. He sees Jesus, falls at his feet, and begs him repeatedly to come and lay his hands on his little daughter. Jesus agrees to his request and goes with him. In Matthew's story the child is already dead. Here, as with Luke, the tension is increased as we read that she is on the point of death. There is an urgency about the request and one expects that there should be no delay in reaching the sick child.

The progress of Jesus to the house of Jairus is slowed down by the crowds pressing in on him. Concealed in the throng of people is the woman with the haemorrhage. Mark stops to describe her: she has been suffering for twelve years, twelve years of the kind of restrictions laid down in Leviticus. She has had no physical contact with any other person. She has been totally isolated. It is clear that she was once a woman of some means as she had consulted many physicians. Now her money is spent and not only is she no better but now she is also destitute. Like Jairus she had heard about Jesus, but whereas he could approach Jesus openly in a public place, she can approach him only in a surreptitious manner. She decides to touch the hem of his cloak. 'If I but touch his clothes I will be made well.' 'Immediately', Mark tells us, the haemorrhage ceased. Then we read that 'she felt in her body that she was healed of her disease'. This somatic knowing does not require any external authority to confirm it. The woman knows, she knows in her body. The immediacy of her healing is matched by the immediacy of the recognition of Jesus that 'power' has gone forth from him, 'Who touched my clothes?' The disciples, whose obtuseness is legendary in Mark, can be excused for finding this question somewhat ludicrous, 'You see the crowd pressing in on you; how can you say, "Who touched me?"' But the woman and Jesus are connected by the intimacy of touch, by the immediacy of their recognition of the exchange of power. Again we are struck by the stress on the initiative of the woman. There is no threat to reveal her identity, but we are told, 'But the woman knowing what had happened to her came in fear and trembling, fell down before him and told him the whole truth.'

Commentators argue about the meaning of 'fear and trembling'. Some who describe the woman in a positive light find it difficult to accommodate what is viewed as a return to a submissive state here. This surprises me. I see nothing submissive about 'fear and trembling' as a response to an intervention of divine grace. In fact it seems the most appropriate response. Angels appear and the recipients of such heavenly messengers invariably bow down in fear and trembling. When Jesus walks on the water the disciples are terrified; likewise when they witness the transfiguration. Terror and amazement seize the women at the tomb and the comment that 'they told no one' is refuted by the Gospel itself! Fear is the prelude to faith — it is a threshold experience marking the boundary between absence and presence, disbelief and belief. The woman who falls at the feet of Jesus and tells him the 'whole truth' recognises the Messiah in the same way as the woman who, confounding the criticism of the disciples, 'wastes' a whole jar of ointment anointing the head of Jesus. In this Gospel where the identity of Jesus remains hidden, the Gospel of the messianic secret, there are several women who 'touch' and 'know'. In the intimacy of that encounter the woman knows who Jesus is and 'in fear and trembling' bows down to acknowledge him. The chosen disciples fail to see, but the outsiders reveal the truth. The man with the unclean spirit dares to name Jesus 'Son of the Most High God'; the woman declared impure dares to touch and know Jesus.

Depending on our perspective we can describe her touching of Jesus as a final act of utter desperation or as an act of profound faith, 'I will be healed', 'I will be saved.' Jesus seems to acknowledge the latter possibility when he responds to her 'whole truth' with, 'Daughter, your faith has made you well.' Her faith is honoured. Her autonomy is respected. Once again I disagree with the implication that calling the woman 'daughter' represents the final 'taming'. The context of the story indicates that this woman has been excluded for twelve years from the community. The appellation 'daughter' welcomes her into a new community, the community of faith, of 'faithful discipleship'. It is of course ironic that 'the twelve' appointed fail to understand, while the woman who has suffered for twelve years demonstrates great faith. Like the Syro-Phoenician woman (Mark 7: 24–30), she initiates healing for others. Later in the Gospel we read that others come and touch 'the fringe of his cloak' and are healed (6: 56). Her faith models the faith required of Jairus, and her healing opens the way for the healing of his daughter. The healings precede the sending out of 'the twelve' and the instructions for discipleship. Yet despite the linking of the narratives through the symbolic number twelve, commentators fail to connect the episodes — ironically similar to the way in which the disciples in their turn had failed to make the connection between the two miracles of the loaves! 'Do you have eyes and fail to see? Do you have ears and fail to hear?' (8: 18)

It is interesting too to observe that whereas Jairus asks that Jesus should 'lay his hands' on his child, the woman reaches out to touch Jesus. She participates in her own healing, in her own salvation. She is not the passive victim of male patronage, or even the object of compassion by a male minister. She draws the power from Jesus by the power of her faith. Of her it could also be said that what she has done should be told 'in memory of her'.

Just as the woman interrupted the story of Jairus, now in turn that story interrupts this one. 'While he was still speaking some people came from the leader's house.' They have come to tell Jairus that his daughter is dead and there is no point 'in troubling the teacher any further'. But the response of Jesus endorses the pattern of the woman's faith, 'Do not fear, only believe.'

The mocking crowds are kept outside and Jesus enters the

house with the parents and 'those who were with him'. He had been asked to lay his hands on the child; instead, he takes her by the hand, a different gesture, the gesture of one accompanying — leading — not dominating. In response the child gets up and walks. We are told that she is twelve years old. Immediately her healing is linked with that of the woman. The girl on the verge of adulthood, about to start menstruating, and the woman who had not ceased to bleed are linked by this blood and this healing. Two untouchable female bodies have been made whole. They are both 'daughters in faith'. There are still boundaries, there are still insiders and outsiders, but the definition of what is 'holy', of what is 'clean', of what is 'pure', has changed. It is faith and not rigid adherence to the letter of the law which opens access to the holy. Salvation is experienced in and through the bodies of women. These women are not simply restored to the community, they constitute a new community, one based on faith. This is why we should attend to the number twelve. Its use here, as in the story of the multiplication of the loaves, has a symbolic significance beyond that of linking the two female characters. The new Israel will include those isolated and rejected by sickness, by impurity, by disease. Faith overcomes even the final separation of death.

Linking the two stories is not merely an interesting literary device but it also symbolises the new inclusive community inaugurated by the ministry of Jesus. The episode of the woman with the haemorrhage interrupts and diverts the course of the healing ministry of Jesus. Just as later in Mark's Gospel another woman, described as a Syro-Phoenician, will challenge Jesus to heal her daughter, here this woman, in claiming power from Jesus, breaks not only the taboos of her exclusion but also the boundaries which demarcate the appropriate channels for healing. It is significant that Jairus is a leader of the synagogue, he understands authority and how it operates. His approach to Jesus is not in the first instance marked by great faith but by respect for the healing ministry of Jesus, and thus he falls at his feet. When the woman enters she does not merely change the course of her own story but that of Jairus as well. She is not motivated by confidence in authority; her experience of the official channels has been entirely negative, she has wasted all her resources. Stripped of all dignity, of all illusion, she is driven simply by faith, 'If I but touch . . .' Her touch becomes the touchstone by which the faith of Jairus will also be measured. The people come to report that his child is dead, he should trouble the teacher no further. It is no longer sufficient to have the confidence of one in authority for another. Jairus is now as vulnerable as the woman, 'Do not fear, only believe.'

The narrator does not tell us that the child is returned to her father, so although Jairus pleaded on behalf of his child there is a sense now in which the child's autonomy is respected, 'He took her by the hand and said to her "Talitha cum", which means "Little girl, get up!" And immediately she got up and began to walk about.' (5: 41, 42) It is as if the young woman may now walk freely in the space cleared for her by the older woman with whose fate and whose faith she has been linked. The Syro-Phoenician woman had to beg for crumbs from the table; here Jesus orders that the girl should be fed, further symbolising and affirming the new life which has been brought to birth.

By interrupting the story of the healing of the daughter of Jairus, the narrator radically transforms it. Instead of a simple healing story it becomes a parable about faith, about inclusiveness, about the in-breaking of the reign of God. It is not simply the story about the healing of two women but about the healing of the imagination which challenges the disciples of Jesus then and now to transcend the restrictions by which they attempt to limit access to divine power. 'And he said to her, "Daughter, your faith has made you well."'

The woman is not simply a model of faith, but her suffering together with the raising of the twelve-year-old girl from the dead prefigures the suffering, death and resurrection of Jesus. Once more we could argue that androcentrism both in the text and in its reception by the believing community has blinded us to this possibility. To see the woman in the image of Christ requires us to make a profound shift in our imaginations which would allow us to see 'the suffering servant' as female:

She was despised and rejected by others;
a woman of suffering and acquainted with infirmity;
and as one from whom others hide their faces,
she was despised and we held her of no account . . . (Isa. 53: 3)

When the sculptor Edwina Sandys created a figure of the crucified Christ as female, as 'Christa', there was a horrified reaction which suggested a paralysis of the imagination.[1] To many this sculpture was scandalous, a form of blasphemy. It was seen as denying the maleness of Jesus instead of being interpreted as extending the capacity of Christ to represent the suffering of women as well as of men. To those surrounding Jesus, the woman's touch was a similar source of scandal. Just as the purity laws were not so much shattered as transcended by the healing exchange between Jesus and the woman, so too our limited perspective on these texts needs to be imaginatively transformed. The context within which we interpret the experience described here is predominantly male; thus the suffering woman cannot prefigure the suffering Christ, our gender blindness limits her potential to act as a symbol in precisely the same way as the blindness of the disciples prevented them from reading the signs presented so clearly to those with eyes of faith.

The woman is described as having suffered greatly, she is rejected by her community, virtually an untouchable. Jesus later warns his disciples that he will 'undergo great suffering and be rejected by the elders, the chief priests and the scribes and be killed and after three days rise again' (8: 31). Peter cannot deal with this idea and is rebuked and further warned that discipleship will involve suffering. The stories about the suffering of the woman and the dying and raising to life of the child comprise a gospel in miniature. The dazzling brightness of faith transfigures the polluting bodies of the women so that they become 'daughters' of God's reign. 'It is to such as these that the kingdom of God belongs.' (10: 14)

CHAPTER 4

DISTURBING WOMEN

Jesus left that place and went away to the district of Tyre and Sidon. Just then a Canaanite woman from that region came out and started shouting, 'Have mercy on me, Lord, Son of David; my daughter is tormented by a demon.' But he did not answer her at all. And his disciples came and urged him, saying, 'Send her away, for she keeps shouting after us.' He answered, 'I was sent only to the lost sheep of the house of Israel.' But she came and knelt before him, saying, 'Lord help me.' He answered, 'It is not fair to take the children's food and throw it to the dogs.' She said, 'Yes, Lord, yet even the dogs eat the crumbs that fall from their master's table.' Then Jesus answered her, 'Woman, great is your faith! Let it be done for you as you wish.' And her daughter was healed instantly. (Matt. 15: 20–8)

There are a number of stories in the Gospels which, despite the best efforts of preachers and teachers to tame them, still send shock waves through the system; this is one. One wonders almost how such a story escaped the original censors of the canon! It disturbs us. It breaks the usual pattern of stiff-necked Pharisees, or foolish disciples blind to the message of Jesus and needing conversion. It breaks the pattern of passive women receiving commendation for listening faithfully. It challenges expectations about the role of Jesus as the one who sees all, who understands all and brings others to insight.

Of course there are attempts to read the story according to the 'appropriate pattern'; so we read that in this story Jesus tests the faith of the woman and once she has revealed her persistent and 'great faith' then her daughter will be cured. In this way the proper role of the woman, her place as an example of 'praying faith' is preserved and the role of Jesus as prophet and healer remains untarnished: a safe woman and a safe Jesus!

I think there are too many 'buts' in the story for such a smooth reading. Perhaps we have to take a risk on an alternative, albeit disturbing interpretation. This story is also told in the Gospel of Mark but I would like to focus on Matthew's version. It is the more immediate telling. Mark reports the story with a combination of direct and indirect speech. Matthew allows the characters to speak for themselves. So we hear the woman addressing Jesus no less than three times, we hear the reaction of the disciples and we hear three responses from Jesus. The mode is direct speech, it is conversation of an engaged and passionate nature. It is a conversation which leads to conversion. At its conclusion no one is left unchanged.

Did Jesus enter the district of Tyre and Sidon or simply approach that gentile territory? It is not absolutely clear. The latter is perhaps suggested by the fact that we read that a woman from that region 'came out'. She comes towards him. We can perhaps imagine a dialogue which takes place on the borders, on the margins. It is of course true that our definition of margin depends on our definition of place, our view of where the centre is. It is clear from what follows that as far as Jesus and the disciples are concerned this is a voice from the edge. She does not have a place, according to the terms of their understanding.

To 'come out' is courageous, whatever the context. There is no threat to the centre when the voices from the edges remain silent. The woman comes out, and more than that, she cries out. She shouts. In Mark's Gospel we read of the blind Bartimaeus who, equally desperate, cries out and is likewise rebuked, here by the disciples, there by the onlookers. (Mark 10: 46–52) Her words are ones now familiar through liturgical usage 'Kyrie Eleison — Lord have mercy.' It is at this point though that the pattern changes. What we expect is a rebuke from Jesus to the onlookers: 'Call him here' (Mark 10: 49), or 'Let her alone.' (Mark 14: 6) In this way the followers of Jesus generally learn that their vision is restricted and that their agenda may not be that shared by Jesus. This time it is different. The disciples' call for the dismissal of the shouting woman is not challenged. Instead it is given a certain rationale. The woman should be dismissed not simply because she is clearly a nuisance and out of

place but more precisely because she has no place. 'I have been
sent only to the lost sheep of the house of Israel.'

We are shocked not merely by the dismissive response but by
the fact that Jesus ignores the woman; his reply is addressed to
the disciples. She doesn't exist for him.

The woman enters her second plea, falling down at his feet. It
is worth remembering that the woman's desperation springs
from her concern for her daughter. We recall the centurion in
Luke's Gospel pleading for his daughter. He at least had the
advantage of his sex and his status. Here the lack of value in
terms of race is compounded by gender: a gentile woman
pleading for her female child.

This time the pleading evokes a response — but what a
shocking one! 'It is not fair to take the children's food and throw
it to the dogs.' The lost sheep of Israel are now 'tenderly
described as 'children' needing to be fed; but the gentiles are
'dogs' to whom food is thrown. As many commentators have
pointed out, the harshness is not even mitigated by the
conciliatory tone of Mark's account, 'Let the children be fed
first.' Feminist scholars trained to be more suspicious are sharper
in their reaction. 'Metaphor or not, Jesus is depicted as
comparing the woman and her daughter to dogs! No churchly
or scholarly gymnastics are able to get around that problem.'[1]

The story reaches its crisis point and turns, or better, is turned
around by the response of the woman. Her retort is immediate
and prefaced neither by shouts nor tears but is almost witty in
its sharpness: 'Yes Lord, but even the dogs eat the crumbs that
fall from their master's table.' The woman takes the imagery
used by Jesus and turns the insult to advantage. 'If you must talk
about dogs. Well, even the dogs are fed.' Her logic counters his.
His exclusive and limited grasp of the possibilities is challenged
by her response. The point is graciously, admiringly conceded,
'Woman, great is your faith.' From the perspective of the
woman, the offer of salvation to the Jews does not mean that
God has excluded the gentiles. It is the woman's faith in God
which is praised. She is the only person in Matthew's Gospel to
receive such an accolade.

The conversation ends. It has indeed been a process of conversion. The woman has achieved her purpose: her daughter is healed. She has changed from a woman begging for mercy to a woman of some authority. She has wrested not just healing for her daughter but respect for herself. Jesus has changed from what appeared to be a position of disengagement, to direct confrontation, to total acceptance. It is ironic that commentators speak of the woman's 'humility' but it is in fact Jesus who demonstrates true humility; he is the one who admits that he was wrong, who recognises her insight.

Ascribing the humility to the woman rather than to Jesus is an understandable reaction from those who are anxious to preserve the status quo: it is the disciples then and now who learn from Jesus; Jesus does not learn from the disciples. Here Jesus is depicted as learning not from a disciple but from a Canaanite woman. We remember the Samaritan woman who was so shocked when asked for a cup of water, 'How is it that you a Jew, ask a drink of me, a woman of Samaria?' (John 4: 9) The shocked response of that woman is mirrored in the shocked responses of commentators who 'know' that it is not possible for Jesus to be instructed by a woman. This is an example of mutual or reciprocal service which in fact is quite characteristic of the ministry of Jesus but which until fairly recently had been forgotten and is now being retrieved.

Justice is not done to the dynamic nature of the encounter or to the vitality of the conversation or particularly to its shocking impact by the description of this woman as 'a model of praying faith'.[2] Other descriptions might be more apt — Sharon Ringe, for example, describes her as 'an uppity woman'![3] This is not simply an example of persistent prayer, 'Ask, and it will be given you, search and you will find' (Matt. 7: 7), but of a case argued and of justice done. The woman's daughter is not healed because, as is so often the case, Jesus has 'compassion', but because he recognises the 'rightness' of her cause. This is the second example in Matthew's Gospel where a woman has asserted her need and has been praised for her faith. In the earlier story the woman with the haemorrhage takes the risk of reaching out to touch. In this story the woman comes out and argues her case. In both instances it is the woman's faith which determines the outcome. These women are not simply passive recipients of grace but active participants in their own salvation. 'Woman, great is your faith. Let it be done for you as you wish.' (Matt. 15: 28) As many commentators have pointed out, this is the greatest praise accorded to anyone in the Gospel. It is not without irony that we recall that a few verses earlier Matthew related Peter's attempt to 'come out' towards Jesus walking on the water but then becoming frightened. 'You of little faith, why did you doubt?'(Matt. 14: 28–31)

In Mark's Gospel this story is followed by the healing of a deaf mute and then the feeding of the four thousand with seven loaves. It is generally agreed that this takes place on gentile territory to parallel the feeding of the five thousand on Jewish soil.

In Matthew's Gospel the gentile references seem more muted but implied as the number seven suggests the nations of Canaan (Cf. Acts 13: 19) and the seven servers (Cf. Acts 6: 5). However something more seems to be at stake.

I find it surprising that the story of the Canaanite woman is not set in the larger context of the feeding narratives in these Gospels. Once again we see the tendency to set the story in brackets. So we find comparisons with the Syro-Phoenician woman in Mark but little attempt to set the story in the wider context. Reading this way the Canaanite woman interrupts the flow. Commentators read on and pick up the pieces. Reading differently, the story of the Canaanite woman assumes a pivotal position. Her story does indeed interrupt the flow but what follows must be read in its light.

If we consider that in the first feeding Israel is fed and that the allusions in the second feeding imply the offer of the heavenly banquet to others, then our question becomes what has made it possible for this banquet to be extended 'to all nations'? (Matt. 28: 19)

At the opening of this chapter we hear the Pharisees and the scribes challenging Jesus. 'Why do your disciples break the tradition of the elders? For they do not wash their hands before they eat?' (Matt. 15: 2) The debate is ostensibly about purity but clearly what is at issue here is not simply how people eat but barriers to common table-fellowship. Are the Pharisees concerned about unwashed hands or are they concerned about gentile contamination?

The encounter with the Canaanite woman continues the debate about table-fellowship. For although her plea is that her daughter should be healed, the conversation turns very quickly to the question of food. 'It is not fair to take the children's food . . .'

Healing and feeding often go together and the link suggested here is worked out in greater detail in the episodes which follow.

The first feeding miracle is preceded by a general healing of those who were sick but this time there is an extraordinary crowd following Jesus: the lame, the maimed, the blind, the mute, and it is precisely these people who are fed. So who do they represent?

Do they represent 'the lost sheep of the house of Israel'? Or does the praise of 'the God of Israel' imply a gentile audience? Whatever way we choose to read it, I suggest that the gentile Canaanite woman has opened the way for a more inclusive understanding of the mission and ministry of Jesus. It is as if a dam has burst, a barrier has broken and the woman in pleading for the healing and feeding of her daughter has opened up healing and table-fellowship to those traditionally barred: the lame, the blind, the mutilated. Whatever way we read it, the apparently domestic scene has wide social ramifications. Jesus, lacking in compassion towards the woman, is challenged by her to rethink his own categories and 'the lost sheep of the house of Israel' become all in need of healing. Jesus is described then as 'filled with compassion' for the crowd and they are fed. We note that once again Matthew adds 'those eating were four thousand *besides women and children*'. It is ironic that a woman and her child have been the catalysts for this feeding which, although it clearly includes women and children, fails to count them! Commentators following this androcentric pattern have also generally failed to 'count' the story in their interpretations of the feeding miracles. So once again removing the brackets around a 'woman's story' releases its extraordinary power.

This is a conversion story, a story about the breaking of boundaries, the shifting of perspective. At its conclusion no character is left unchanged. The disciples have also had to go through their own conversion process. Prior to the first feeding they had urged Jesus, 'Send the crowds away', and repeated that demand in relation to the shouting woman, 'Send her away.' Now they become the ones called to distribute the food to all who had gathered on the mountain.

But what of the woman? Of course her situation has changed. The purpose for which she came has been achieved. She has become an important symbol of resistance, of perseverance, of great faith. So for contemporary women she becomes an interesting model. She provides us with a clear example of 'talking back to the tradition'. It is worth observing how that process of change occurs. At first we hear the woman shouting, 'Have mercy on me.' This sounds like a cry of utter desperation. We can imagine that the shouting gives way to weeping as she comes and kneels. 'Lord help me.' Then comes the turning point of the story. The woman takes the image used by Jesus and turns it to her favour. Pleading and lament yield to sharp wit. Sandra Schneiders talks of women who 'use the master's tools to dismantle the master's house';[4] this woman uses the master's imagery to destroy the master's argument. The very words used to exclude are turned, are subverted, until they become the principle of inclusion.

To read this story from the woman's perspective allows her the role of the protagonist. From being perceived as the object of concern or indeed of annoyance to be dismissed she becomes the subject of the story. From a position of being subject to external authorities she becomes the author of the script. She refuses to be defined in terms of her exclusion, to be defined by what is not permitted, and instead risks all for the sake of what could be possible. She dares to imagine differently. The disciples attempted to put this woman in what they consider to be her place. Jesus had no place for her in his plan; but this woman demonstrates that she indeed knows her true place and she takes it.

Of course it is not possible to translate directly from the context of 2,000 years ago into our contemporary situation. On the other hand it is equally impossible to ignore our present experience when reading such ancient but classic scripts. We read them as living words, or rather we read them asking whether they continue to be words of life. This story I suggest can once again function as a liberating word for women if we read it both suspiciously and hopefully. We read suspiciously when we question the interpretation which attempts to domesticate the text and smooth over its offensive language, its scandalous tone. We read hopefully when we negotiate our way between the pain and the promise of the story. This is a tale of great faith, indeed, of faith which overcomes rejection, denial, silence, opposition, and which persists. In this tale we have a woman who reflects back the image of Christ. It is as if momentarily the woman is given the lines which we expect to come from the mouth of Jesus; she becomes the one through whom God's reign is revealed. The story truly yields up its blessing!

CHAPTER 5

FEEDING WOMEN

When he went ashore, he saw a great crowd and he had compassion for them and cured their sick. When it was evening, the disciples came to him and said, 'This is a deserted place, and the hour is late; send the crowds away so that they may go into the villages and buy food for themselves.' Jesus said to them, 'They need not go away; you give them something to eat.' They replied, 'We have nothing here but five loaves and two fish.' And he said, 'Bring them here to me.' Then he ordered the crowds to sit down on the grass. Taking the five loaves and the two fish, he looked up to heaven, and blessed and broke the loaves and gave them to the disciples and the disciples gave them to the crowds. And all ate and were filled; and they took up what was left over of the broken pieces, twelve baskets full. And those who ate were about five thousand men, besides women and children. (Matt. 14: 14–21)

After Jesus had left that place, he passed along the sea of Galilee, and he went up the mountain, where he sat down. Great crowds came to him bringing with them the lame, the maimed, the blind, the mute, and many others. They put them at his feet, and he cured them, so that the crowd was amazed when they saw the mute speaking, the maimed whole, the lame walking, and the blind seeing. And they praised the God of Israel.
Then Jesus called his disciples and said, 'I have compassion for the crowd, because they have been with me now for three days and have nothing to eat; and I do not want to send them away hungry for they might faint on the way.' The disciples said to him, 'Where are we to get enough bread in the desert to feed so great a crowd?' Jesus asked them, 'How many loaves have you?' They said, 'Seven and a few small fish.' Then ordering the crowd to sit down on the ground, he took the seven loaves and the fish; and after giving thanks he broke them and gave them

to the disciples and the disciples gave them to the crowds. And all of them ate and were filled; and they took up the broken pieces left over, seven baskets full. Those who had eaten were four thousand men, besides women and children. (Matt. 15: 29–38)

All four Gospels include at least one feeding story. Matthew and Mark have two. Matthew's Gospel is the only one to mention women and children. As we noted in the previous chapter the women and children are not included in the counting, but are mentioned in addition to, 'besides' the men. How do we view this 'addition'? One commentator suggests that 'By adding this phrase to Mark 6: 44, Matthew enlarges the number of people affected by the multiplication, thus making it even more spectacular.'[1] Other commentators agree that this addition makes the miracle a significant social event possibly bringing the number up to twenty thousand. So are we dealing simply with numbers? Women and children swell the number of those fed, of the assembly gathered, but are of no further interest. I think that these commentators miss the point. I don't think that Matthew is playing a numbers game; for example, he does not increase the number of baskets which are filled with the leftover pieces and logic would surely demand this if we are to imagine a much larger crowd of 'twenty to thirty thousand'. The commentators miss the precise point Matthew is making: he does not add on the women and children in order to suggest an even larger gathering. They are not subsumed into the large crowd — which would have been the effect if he had been concerned to portray an even more spectacular event. Matthew is not interested in counting the women and children but in drawing our attention to their presence.

In the other Gospels it is possible — indeed very likely — that we are supposed to imagine that women as well as men are present among such a large crowd. After all we know of the presence of women and children in the crowds who come for healing. They are there but perhaps because it was not customary for women and children to eat with men they are not 'counted in'. Mark, for example, describes the seating arrangements as sitting in groups, *symposia*. The symposium was a fraternal gathering and if women were present they were there specifically as entertainers. So despite the fact that the feeding takes place in the open air, Mark suggests a formal banquet arrangement in order to image the heavenly banquet. So perhaps we have to imagine that the women are seated separately and thus not counted in the formal groups, present but invisible, subsumed under the usual 'for us men', or if visible, like their children, they are seen and not heard — if heard they are not counted. Against such a background Matthew's mention of the women is indeed startling. Matthew reminds us that women and children are present; they may not be counted, but for the Matthean community they count. Their presence is highlighted to signal the difference in the community constituted by discipleship. 'And pointing to the disciples, he said, "Here are my mother and my brothers! For whoever does the will of my father in heaven is my brother and sister and mother."'(12: 49–50)

Women who read the Scriptures are like the Canaanite woman searching for the crumbs which have fallen from the table. I think that the crumbs gathered from this feeding of women and children will indeed fill a basket.

Context alters text. Commentators generally alert readers to the Eucharistic references in the feeding — it points forward to the Last Supper and beyond. It is usual to point out the contrast between Herod's banquet, which immediately precedes this passage, and the banquet offered by Jesus. The feedings are set in the context of the 'little faith' of the disciples (Matt. 14: 31; 16: 8).[2]

I want to frame the feedings in the following way:

Herod's birthday party and the dance of the daughter of Herodias (14: 6–11)
The first feeding (14: 13–21)
The Canaanite woman and her daughter (15: 21–8)
The second feeding (15: 29–38)

The house of Simon and the woman with an alabaster jar
(26: 6–13)
The third feeding: the Passover (26: 14–29).

I want to suggest a type of step parallelism in the narrative as the
understanding of the significance of the bread blessed, broken
and given out, grows with each feeding. All three 'feasts' are
prefaced by stories which relate to the presence of women at
meals. It is also clear to me that, despite the efforts of the author
we call Matthew, commentators may look but often still fail to
see the women at these crucial ventures. One could transpose to
them the question of Jesus to the uncomprehending disciples,
'You of little faith . . . Do you still not perceive?' An androcentric
reading, as noted above, does not attach any significance to the
presence of women; such a reading may draw our attention, for
example, to the 'little faith' of Peter (14: 31) but fails to
mention, let alone see any comparison with the 'great faith' of
the Canaanite woman! (15: 28)[3]
   The banquet to celebrate the birthday of Herod stands in
sharp contrast to the banquet for the people hosted by Jesus.
Herod, the Tetrarch, links Jesus with John the Baptist, thus
implying that the same fate may await Jesus. He wishes to have
John killed as the prophet has criticised his relationship with
Herodias, the wife of Philip, his brother. Tellingly John is
reported as saying 'You cannot have her' (14: 4) — the woman
belongs to the man. In Mark's account it is Herodias who bears
a grudge against John and wishes to have him put to death, but
is prevented from doing so because Herod is interested in John's
teaching. This is not the case in Matthew's account where Herod
himself desires John's death. The daughter of Herodias is
described as dancing 'in their midst' and pleasing Herod.
Women are clearly present both as entertainers (the daughter)
and guests (the mother), when the head of John the Baptist is
brought on a dish and given to the daughter, who in turn gives
it to her mother — a gruesome offering. The responsibility of
the women for the death of John the Baptist is mitigated by
Matthew's stress on the actions and motives of Herod Antipas

himself — whose regret seems fairly shallow — but one can hardly regard their presence and participation in this anti-banquet, this travesty of hospitality, as anything other than negative.

With relief we turn to the banquet hosted by Jesus where women and children are present, not to entertain the guests, but to be offered healing and nourishment. When Jesus sees the crowd he has compassion for them and cures their sick. The reign of God bringing life contrasts sharply with the dealing in death of the rule of Herod. The crowd is asked to recline, but not in ordered groups, serried ranks of men, as in Mark, but apparently as a family grouping. The meal offered anticipates the setting of the Passover. In both cases it is evening (14: 15; 26: 20). In both cases the procedure is the same: Jesus takes, blesses, breaks and gives the bread to the disciples (14: 19; 26: 26). In turn the disciples give it to the people, all eat and are satisfied. The messianic feast hosted by Wisdom's prophet includes not only five thousand men but also women and children. Indeed later in the Gospel when the disciples, true to form, try to send away those who are bringing their children, they are reprimanded, 'Let the little children come to me and do not stop them; for it is to such as these that the kingdom of God belongs.' (19: 14) It is thus ironic that neither the disciples nor their contemporary counterparts attend to the places laid at this feast for women and for children.

I explored the story of the Canaanite woman in the previous chapter but I am returning to it here to highlight the link with the feeding narratives. The first feeding of the five thousand is followed by the story of Peter walking on the water and becoming fearful. He is reprimanded for his 'little faith'. There follows a discussion about washing and defilement and once again Peter is portrayed as requiring further explanation. Then we have the story of the Canaanite woman which forms a preface to the second feeding in the same way as the banquet of Herod provided the backdrop against which we read the first feeding.

In Matthew's account the daughter of Herodias did not enter

the banquet but was already present 'in the midst'; this woman 'comes out'. She does not belong. From the beginning her presence is disturbing. She shouts after the disciples. A noisy raucous woman, she should be dismissed. The disciples are slow to learn; they had also wanted to dismiss the crowd which followed Jesus: 'Send the crowds away' and now 'Send her away.' Both requests are ignored. As already discussed, it is not only the disciples who need to be converted, but Jesus himself. The point I want to stress again here is that the initiative belongs to the woman. This woman is described neither as daughter nor wife, she is beholden to no man. She is the subject of the story. Her plea on behalf of her daughter provides us with the redemptive counterfoil to Herodias and her daughter. In that case a daughter pleaded on behalf of her mother for a life to be taken. Here a mother pleads on behalf of her daughter for a life to be saved, for her child to be healed. The crumbs taken up from the feeding of the five thousand, besides women and children, are needed by another woman and her child. The apparently all-inclusive banquet in the desert place had its limits which are now being challenged by this woman laying her claim to the leftovers!

The insight of the woman marks her as a Wisdom figure whose daring words are justified by her children. Jesus concedes the argument and graciously accedes to the woman's request, which contrasts with Herod's apparently reluctant acquiescence with the request of the daughter of Herodias. The woman's affective reasoning opens the path for the gentiles, clearing a space at the table. She is commended for her 'great faith'. We are reminded of the amazement of Jesus at the faith of the centurion, '. . . in no one in Israel have I found such faith' (8: 10). The 'little faith' of the disciples is set against such 'great faith'. Their limited understanding is contrasted with her greater understanding. Far from seeking further explanation, as Peter does, she herself answers the objection. 'Even the dogs eat the crumbs that fall from the master's table.' (15: 21)

Thus it is the woman who sets the scene for the second feeding. Jesus is described, typically in Matthew, as going up a mountain. Great crowds come 'bringing with them the lame, the maimed, the blind, the mute and many others' (14: 29). So instead of a generalised 'healing of the sick', here we have a very specific, indeed graphic, description of those in need of healing, those who would represent the excluded ones. The emphasis appears to be on 'the lost sheep' of the house of Israel rather than on the gathering in of the gentiles. There is some ambiguity here as those healed are described as 'praising the God of Israel'(15: 31).

A second feeding only makes sense as a development of the first, an extension of that invitation to those on the outside whether by reason of race or deformity. These are the people who need to be fed. The disciples may be slow but they have learnt one lesson — they no longer request that the crowd be sent away and merely ask where the food should be obtained. Once again, although fish is mentioned, the emphasis is on the breaking and sharing of bread. The disciples receive the bread and give it to the crowds. This time seven baskets of pieces left over are taken up in contrast to the twelve baskets at the first feeding (which represented the twelve tribes of Israel). Once again men, women and children are present, but this time their inclusion is not surprising — the Canaanite woman has ensured the inclusiveness of the hospitality which now extends, not only to women and children, but to the once mute who now speak, the lame who now walk, and the blind who now see. This is truly a foretaste of the eschatological banquet, 'On the mountain, the Lord of hosts will prepare for all peoples, a feast of rich food . . . And he will destroy on this mountain the shroud that is cast over all peoples . . .' (Isa. 25: 6–7)

The feast is for all peoples. Matthew's feasts embody the egalitarian principle expressed in Paul's letter to the Galatians, 'There is no longer Jew or Greek, there is no longer slave or free, there is no longer male or female, for you are all one in Christ Jesus.' (Gal. 3: 27) The first feeding is not repudiated but extended. The opening out of the meal to include and name women and children already implies that the *oikos*, the 'household' of God has a different economy to that of the social world around it. The Canaanite woman pushes open the door even further so that it is not just the *oikos* of Israel which is fed but the house of the gentiles also. Those 'little in body' are healed and fed in that extraordinary and poignant image of the pilgrim journey up the mountain of the maimed, the blind, the lame and the mute. 'I have compassion for these people.'

The Eucharistic references in the two feedings are so clear that we are justified in connecting the Passover meal to both feedings. I have decided to make this link even more explicit by referring to the 'last supper' in Matthew's Gospel as 'the third feeding'. Like the other two, it is prefaced by a story concerning a woman. Mark's version of this story of the woman who anoints the head of Jesus is discussed in detail in Chapter six, but the point here is to link the stories of the three women who provide foils to the feeding narratives in this Gospel. Like the daughter of Herodias, this woman performs her action in a house in the midst of a meal, 'as he sat at table'. Like the Canaanite woman, she approaches Jesus, 'a woman came to him', and initiates the action. As in the story of the Canaanite woman, the disciples object, 'Why this waste?' This time it is Jesus who defends the actions of the woman, who does not speak. However the words of praise spoken about her match those spoken of the Canaanite woman: there we had 'great faith'; here we have 'what she has done will be told in remembrance of her'. In a travesty of generosity the daughter of Herodias offered the head of John the Baptist to her mother; here this woman anoints the head of Jesus with a gesture so utterly extravagant that it too sends shock waves of astonishment among those present. Just as the Canaanite woman redeemed the mother/daughter relationship, here the unnamed woman redeems the extravagant gesture. The evil work of Herod is met by the 'good work' of the woman. John the Baptist is beheaded; here the head of Jesus is anointed and prepared for burial.

But the woman performing her act of service for Jesus is not merely a foil for the daughter of Herodias performing her act of disservice for John, she is also a foil for the disciples. The 'great faith' of the Canaanite woman is both a contrast to and a measure for the 'little faith' of the male disciples. Here the 'good work' of the woman, in recognising who Jesus is, and daringly preparing him for his burial, contrasts with the betrayal of Judas and the weakness of Peter. Encircled by the conspiring of the elders and the chief priests, and the treachery of Judas, the beautiful act of the woman gives witness to another possibility. Judas is willing to betray Jesus for thirty pieces of silver; the woman is willing to waste 'very costly ointment which could have been sold for a large sum'. The act of betrayal is met and transcended by an act of greater love. Thus the woman pouring out the costly ointment prefigures the outpouring of the life of Jesus for his disciples. This daughter of Wisdom is justified by her deeds (Matt. 11: 19) and what she has done will be told in memory of her.

Against this backdrop the third and final feeding takes place. The story of the woman is framed by conspiracy, by threats of violence. The story of the last feeding is set in the frame of the betrayal of Judas and the predicted denial of Peter. In the midst of this there is a different dance, not this time the dance of death, but in the midst of death, denial and desertion there is the dance of life: the bread is blessed, broken and given out, even to those who will betray and desert. The way of violence and death is met by compassion and love. Once again Wisdom is justified by her deeds.

The table of Jesus is Wisdom's table — a table laid before us even in the midst of our foes. The stories of the women who preface these feedings define the territory for us, or to hold to the feeding metaphor, they prepare the table. In the first story this is a negative example, a counter-story against which the other banquets are set. The anti-symbol of the head of John the Baptist is finally redeemed and transfigured by the self-gift of Jesus to his disciples, 'Take, eat; this is my body.' The Canaanite woman and the unnamed woman prepare for the feedings of the 'little ones' and the ones of 'little faith'. They act as foils for the uncomprehending disciples and offer models of true and faithful discipleship. More than that though, they prefigure the acts of Jesus. Women and children are not counted in simply to swell

the numbers, but their presence alerts us to the true nature of
the reign of God, the inclusive reign of Wisdom[4] in whose
memory the gospel is preached.

> Wisdom has built her house
> she has hewn her seven pillars
> she has slaughtered her animals
> she has mixed her wine,
> she has set her table.
> She has sent out her servant girls
> she calls
> from the highest places in the
> town.
> You that are simple, turn in
> here!
> To those without sense she says,
> Come eat of my bread
> and drink of the wine I have
> mixed.
> Lay aside foolishness and live,
> and walk in the way of insight.
> (Prov. 9: 1–6)

CHAPTER 6

REMEMBERING WOMEN

While he was at Bethany in the house of Simon the leper, as he sat at the table, a woman came with an alabaster jar of very costly ointment of nard, and she broke open the jar and poured the ointment on his head. But some were there who said to one another in anger, 'Why was this ointment wasted in this way? For this ointment could have been sold for more than three hundred denarii and the money given to the poor.' And they scolded her. But Jesus said, 'Let her alone, why do you trouble her? She has performed a good service for me. For you always have the poor with you, and you can show kindness to them whenever you wish; but you will not always have me. She has done what she could; she has anointed my body beforehand for its burial. Truly I tell you wherever the good news is proclaimed in the whole world what she has done will be told in remembrance of her.' (Mark 14: 3–9)

'What she has done will be told in memory of her.' What extraordinary words! This woman will be remembered, her story will be told throughout the whole world. We are startled by the fact that it is *her* memory which is to be kept. But how does one hold the memory of a nameless woman? Not easily, it seems.

Sometime ago I was preparing to discuss this story with an adult education group, about sixty in number, who were pursuing a course in theology. I quoted the last line and asked whether anyone could place the text. There was silence. Then one man said that he was reminded of the Last Supper; did it belong there? He was interrupted by another speaker who suggested that this was a feminist distortion of that familiar text! 'Well, if it was', I responded, perhaps too gleefully, 'then Jesus was the feminist!'

The anecdote reveals very clearly what has been described as a kind of collective amnesia on the part of the Church in relation to women. Here it is most vividly illustrated as the explicit instruction for *anamnesis*, remembrance, is forgotten!

So much ink has been spilled over the precise meaning of the words in Luke's Gospel, 'Do this in remembrance of me' (Luke 22: 19), but until the efforts of feminist scholars raised awareness[1] this story had failed to touch the popular imagination and had certainly failed to influence pastoral practice. We remember the name of the betrayer of Jesus, which follows immediately after the anointing episode: the story of Judas is narrated several times during the Church's preparation for Easter and Irish custom has popularly named Spy Wednesday in his memory; but although the story of the anointing continues to be told, there is no day set apart 'in memory of her'. The memory has not been carried. Even in situations where the story is recalled, people generally have difficulty placing it in context. In another revealing incident I asked a group of women what they remembered about the story of the woman anointing Jesus. 'She was a sinner, a prostitute', one suggested. 'Was she Mary Magdalene?' another asked. 'Jesus showed his great love by forgiving her.' So what has happened? Where does this version of the story come from? All four Gospels carry a story about the anointing of Jesus by an unnamed woman. The one which has dominated the imagination is Luke's story (Luke 7: 36–50). It is Luke, and only Luke, who describes the woman as a sinner, yet this telling has powerfully coloured all other versions and left its mark even on the earlier text of Mark! It is with some irony that we realise that Luke's version is not part of the passion narrative and does not include the injunction to 'remember'!

So I want to look at the text as we read it in Mark's Gospel, to retrieve that reading from its Lucan stranglehold and set it apart, set it within its own frame. Having done that, I want to ask how we might remain faithful to the instruction to hold this story in living memory today.

This is a very visual text. It reads almost like a set of stage directions. We have a place, Bethany. We have a person, Simon, in whose house the action takes place. He is described as 'Simon the leper'. We know nothing more of this Simon. We presume that he was cured of his leprosy, perhaps by Jesus, which would provide the excuse for the banquet. But Simon is not the focus of the story. Despite this he is described and named. Then we have Jesus who is sitting, or better, reclining at table. Now the set is ready for the entrance of the woman. She is not identified by name or even by the usual context which would be her relationship to a male. She is not 'the daughter of . . .' or 'the wife of . . .'

She is described by her actions. She has come carrying an alabaster jar of very expensive perfume which she breaks open and pours over the head of Jesus. Now watch the reaction of the guests. 'Why was the ointment wasted in this way? For this ointment could have been sold for more than three hundred denarii and the money given to the poor.' What has upset these people? It is not the presence of the woman which causes surprise or anger. This would suggest that this was not such an unusual occurrence. Women not present at the meal could be there in the capacity of entertainer.[2] However the fact that the guests have no problem with the actual presence of the woman should inhibit us from describing her in any way as 'unvirtuous', as a prostitute or a sinner. The text leaves no opening for such an interpretation. But the guests are angry and their anger is directed in a typically self-righteous way at the waste: the money should have been given to the poor. They rebuke the woman.

This tone of righteousness is familiar. Anyone who steps out of bounds is chastised: the blind Bartimaeus who shouted out was sternly ordered to be quiet (Mark 10: 48); the disciples rebuked those bringing children to Jesus (Mark 10: 13); and of course the practices of Jesus himself were criticised by the Pharisees, 'Why does he eat with tax-collectors and sinners?' (Mark 2: 16) These people are 'out of control' and so they threaten the existing order. They disrupt and disturb. They must be corrected.

In our story it is the utter extravagance of the woman which is so threatening. The whole jar is wasted. This is not about a few miserable trickles of oil, the kind of gesture used in impoverished liturgies where the one presiding stops to explain what the drip of oil or drop of water symbolises! This is not a safe minimalist gesture, this is an act of pure embarrassing madness: a whole jar of precious, very expensive ointment is poured out! Imagine too the increase in horror and protest had the guests known what we, Mark's readers, know — this man is about to die. What a waste of resources!

Context alters the text: Jesus from his perspective reads the act of the woman quite differently. The NRSV gives us a very prosaic rendering: 'She has performed a good service for me.' The RSV uses the phrase, 'She has done a beautiful thing.' The Greek word *kalos* can be translated either as 'good' or 'beautiful'. However we express it, the meaning is clear: the outrageous act has become something quite other — a good work. The woman who, a few moments previously was the object of reprimand, is now praised and with an extravagance to match her gesture, 'Truly I tell you, wherever the good news is proclaimed in the whole world, what she has done will be told in remembrance of her.' A reckless gesture translated into an act of passionate love, a beautiful work.

So what is the context which so alters the text or the act for Jesus? Jesus in his response does, what I want to suggest, is necessary for all episodes concerning women in the Gospels: he sets the action on to a much larger stage. I described the story earlier in terms of a little scene in a drama: the stage is set, the main actors are present and then, 'Woman enters left.' At the end of her scene she exits, she has not even been named. We will not hear of her again. It is, one might say, a bit part. You would not make your name playing this role! And yet something has changed utterly. Otherwise how can we explain the inappropriate response of Jesus matching the inappropriate gesture of the woman?

The comment about the poor has tended to concern commentators who are anxious to speak in terms of 'Jesus' option for the poor'. This is an awkward text. It is useful though as a constant reminder that we cannot manipulate the Gospel for our purposes. The Jesus portrayed in the Gospels escapes every pigeon-hole into which we put him. This saying seems to parallel the reply of Jesus to the criticism that the disciples of

John fast, whereas the followers of Jesus feast. 'The wedding guests cannot fast while the bridegroom is with them, can they? . . . The days will come when the bridegroom is taken away from them.' (Mark 2: 20) Here Jesus tells the listeners, 'You will not always have me.' There is plenty of time for good works and for fasting but right now something else has taken precedence. It is a misreading of the text to argue that the importance of caring for the poor is undermined. We are at a moment of crisis, a turning point, and the woman recognises it, she who knows the bridegroom. It is time for the feast. In anointing the head of Jesus she recognises him as the Christ, the anointed one. Jesus praises the woman's foresight. She has anointed his body for burial but he also recognises her insight into his identity, 'What she has done will be told in memory of her.' We are reminded of an earlier episode in the Gospel where Jesus asked, 'Who do the people say that I am?' (8: 27) When Peter names Jesus as the Messiah but refuses to accept that 'the Son of man must undergo great suffering and be killed', he is severely rebuked. He described Jesus as 'the anointed one' without understanding the implications of what he was saying. In contrast the woman says nothing but her sign/action is prophetic and so she is greatly praised. Her act anticipates not only the death but also the resurrection of Jesus, the recognition of Jesus as the Christ. What is implicit in her action is made explicit in the words of the centurion, 'Truly this man was the son of God.' (15: 39) The outsiders speak the truth. Those apparently on the inside, the disciples, the invited guests, consistently fail to comprehend.

So the apparently private, idiosyncratic act breaks out into the public arena. Its political significance can only be recognised by attending to the context. So let us look at the story within different frames. The first frame is provided by the placing of the story within Mark's text. Chapter 14 begins:

> It was two days before the Passover and the festival of Unleavened Bread. The chief priests and the scribes were looking for a way to arrest Jesus by stealth and kill him; for they said, 'Not during the festival, or there may be a riot among the people.' (14: 1–2)

The story of the anointing at Bethany follows, and then we read:

> *Then Judas Iscariot who was one of the twelve, went to the
> chief priests in order to betray him to them. When they heard it
> they were greatly pleased, and promised to give him money. So
> he began to look for an opportunity to betray him. (14: 10–11)*

Several times throughout the text of this book I refer to the
practice of reading the stories about women as stories 'in
brackets'. This is a perfect example. Place brackets around the
story of the anointing and the text flows freely from the notion
of arresting Jesus to the offer of Judas. To prove the point this is
precisely what happens in the Gospel of Luke. There is no
anointing story to interrupt the process or the flow (Luke 22:
1–6). So how do we read Mark's text? Do we keep brackets
around this story and allow it to take its place as a subtext, a
minor scene in a major drama? What function does it have?
Does it interrupt the process, as the Lucan editing suggests, or is
it an integral part of the action that follows?

Our text is framed between the threat to kill Jesus and the
betrayal of Jesus. In John's Gospel this is rendered in sensuous
terms, the stench of death contrasting with the scent of perfume
filling the whole house (John 12: 3). But this is Mark! Mark has
interrupted his stories before. One example is the raising of the
daughter of Jairus which is held up, as it were, by the healing of
the woman with the haemorrhage (5: 22–34). In that case it is
clear that the threads can be woven together forming a richer
tapestry of meaning.[3]

What are we dealing with here? A story of betrayal interrupted
by an act of extravagant love? A tale of death interrupted by a
glimpse of resurrection? Economic matters affect both tales: on
the one hand we have the total disregard of resources by the
woman who wastes the equivalent of 300 times the daily wage
of a labourer; on the other hand we have the bargaining of Judas
for his fee. Ironically, while Judas attempts to put a price on the
head of Jesus, the woman by the utter extravagance of her
gesture indicates clearly that this is not possible. Her action

transcends the logic of a normal transaction and moves into another realm, the realm of grace, of gratuitous love. The supper at Bethany and the supper with the disciples are both framed by threats of betrayal: 'One of you will betray me' (14: 18) and 'This night . . . you will deny me three times.' (14: 30) Caught between fear and betrayal are these acts of self-giving. So the action of the woman anticipates the self-giving of Jesus, 'Take, this is my body.' It is interesting to note that Mark includes no injunction to remember or indeed repeat this act! It is Luke who includes the phrase 'in remembrance of me' in his supper narrative (Luke 22: 19).

Read in this way the story of the anointing woman does not interrupt the passion narrative but provides a means of interpreting it. The gesture of the unnamed woman gives us a model of discipleship, a measure by which the other actors in this drama are judged. Her generous impulse contrasts with the haggling of Judas, her love and compassion with his betrayal, her insight with the blindness of the disciples, her exposed actions with the stealth of the chief priests. Finally of course her recognition of Jesus as Messiah, the anointed one, gives the readers the correct frame of reference for understanding the ensuing events.

There is another way we can read the story which consolidates this idea of the episode as a reference point for the passion. Chapter 13 contains the teaching of Jesus concerning the end of the world. He warns his disciples about the suffering which they will endure and he urges patience and watchfulness.

This prologue to the passion narrative is framed by two episodes describing the actions of unnamed women. Both stories depict apparently foolish gestures which are taken up and interpreted differently by Jesus. In the first story Jesus is sitting watching a crowd putting money into the treasury. A poor widow comes and puts in two small copper coins. In contrast to the anointing with expensive perfume, this apparently insignificant act would have gone unremarked had not Jesus called his disciples, 'Truly I tell you this poor widow has put in more than all those who are contributing to the treasury. For all of them have contributed out of their abundance; but she out of her poverty has put in everything she had, all she had to live on.' (12: 43)

The stories intersect at the point of radical giving. Both women give all. It is of no consequence whether the 'all' is a jar of spikenard or two copper coins. They give not out of their surplus but their whole living, and in so doing anticipate the whole self-giving and radical love of Jesus, 'Take, this is my body.'

In both cases the actions of the women are set against a background which favourably contrasts their behaviour with that of the scribes. In the first case the scribes are seeking 'the best seats in the synagogues, the places of honour at banquets. They devour widows' houses and for the sake of appearance say long prayers.' (12: 39–40) In the next story they are plotting to kill Jesus. The women, whose actions are either ignored, as is the widow, or condemned, as in the case of the anointing woman, are the ones who are raised up as models of discipleship. 'Truly I tell you . . . she has put in everything . . .' 'Truly I tell you . . . what she has done will be told in memory of her.'

Two unnamed women, two 'inserted' stories to be read as 'beautiful' tales or to be read as gospels in miniature. These are stories which both gather up what has preceded them and anticipate what is to follow; they form a touchstone on which the passion can be read and understood and a marker by which discipleship can be measured. Once more we watch as the brackets or insertion points around 'women's stories' are removed, and these apparently minor episodes break their boundaries and become prophetic.

Because I do not want to dilute the power of this story or diminish its potential to be remembered, I will not refer to the other versions at this point. Suffice to note that Matthew places the episode in the same position as Mark and with almost identical wording. Once again there is no reference to sinfulness. There is no qualification to the positive approval by Jesus, 'What she has done will be told in memory of her.' (Matt. 26: 6–13)

So how should we tell this story? How can that memory be

recovered for the contemporary Christian community? Is it sufficient to peel off the overlay, the layers of paint, from Luke's vivid picture and allow Mark's portrait to stand separately?

It is the first step. Conflating the stories in the Gospels dilutes their power and generally presents us with a bland Jesus and a set of generalised instructions. Recognising the plurality in the tradition can facilitate us as we explore the possibilities of living with the ambiguities and pluralities of our own time.

In this case however something more is at stake: a memory vital to the history of women in the Christian community has been forgotten. Retrieving this memory can be part of the process which enables women to find their roots in the Christian tradition and to explore possibilities for the discipleship of women today.

This story challenges us on a number of levels. In the first place it challenges those who attempt to diminish the role of women or who fail to recognise the significance of their discipleship. Secondly it challenges those who believe that women must reject the tradition because of its predominantly male perspective. The irony of Mark's Gospel is that it is not the named male disciples who model the correct response to Jesus, but outsiders, including these unnamed women.

To restore this story to living memory allows it to function as an imaginative resource to nourish possibilities for the future. To tell this woman's story keeps alive not just her memory but a way of discipleship. Stories such as these, if read as isolated or discrete episodes in the life of Jesus, are diluted of their power. They are domesticated and rendered harmless. But when they are read in context the words crack open dangerously, prophetically, powerfully. Remember it was not just a few drops of perfume trickling down but a whole jar broken open, spilling over, poured out!

CHAPTER 7

CONFRONTING WOMEN

While Peter was below in the courtyard one of the servant girls of the high priest came by. When she saw Peter warming himself, she stared at him and said, 'You were also with Jesus, the man from Nazareth.' But he denied it saying, 'I do not know or understand what you are talking about.' And he went out into the forecourt. Then the cock crowed. And the servant girl on seeing him, began to say to the bystanders, 'This man is one of them.' But again he denied it. Then after a little while the bystanders again said to Peter, 'Certainly you are one of them; for you are a Galilean.' But he began to curse and he swore an oath, 'I do not know this man you are talking about.' At that moment the cock crowed for the second time. Then Peter remembered that Jesus had said to him, 'Before the cock crows twice, you will deny me three times.' And he broke down and wept. (Mark 14: 66–72)

Of course this is Peter's story. He is the subject. The narrator places him centre stage, the spotlight picks him out below in the courtyard and catches him at the end when he breaks down in tears. The maid is merely a foil. She has a 'bit part'. We know this and are reminded of it when the scripts for the liturgical reading of the passion story on Passion Sunday and on Good Friday are handed out, and her part is read along with several others marked 'O'. Occasionally the same speaker reads both parts of the dialogue, obscuring her role even further. Peter is of course the anti-hero of this story; we have a context in which to place him. But what of the maidservant, the female slave? Is she an isolated character? Does she too have a context? Does she simply appear and disappear without trace?

First of all we need to situate the story of the denial of Peter. All the gospel writers — apart from Luke — interweave the hearing of Jesus before the high priest with the questioning of Peter. In Mark the stories are told in parallel: Jesus is taken to the high priest; Peter has followed at a distance and is described as sitting with the guards 'warming himself at the fire' (14: 54). Then follows the trial of Jesus. The testimony of the witnesses is not reliable and Jesus is questioned, 'Have you no answer?' At first he is silent and then the high priest asks him, 'Are you the Messiah, the Son of the Blessed One?' To this Jesus replies 'I am; and you will see the Son of Man, seated at the right hand of the Power, and coming with the clouds of heaven.' (14: 62) This declaration is immediately followed by the condemnation and beating of Jesus.

The scene then changes to the courtyard below and the dialogue with Peter. It is worth recalling Peter's involvement the last time in the Gospel that a discussion about the identity of Jesus took place: '"But who do you say that I am?" Peter answered him, "You are the Messiah." And he sternly ordered them not to tell anyone about him.' (8: 29–30) Jesus then explains to the disciples that 'the Son of Man must undergo great suffering and be rejected by the elders, the chief priests and the scribes, and be killed and after three days rise again' (8: 31). Peter, who clearly found this description difficult to reconcile with his notion of 'Messiah', protests and is sharply rebuked and Jesus goes on to preach his paradoxical gospel of reversals. 'For those who want to save their life will lose it and those who lose their life for my sake and for the sake of the gospel will save it.' (8: 35) Peter's memory is short, or he is — at least according to this narrator — particularly obtuse. Not alone did he forget or misunderstand that teaching, but having insisted 'Even though I must die with you I will not deny you' (14: 31), this is precisely what he does. In each of these conversations Peter's dialogue partner is Jesus. In a sense it is Peter who, playing the role of the fool, acts as a foil to enable Jesus to reveal the truth about himself. Mary Ann Tolbert, commenting on the part played by the apparently dim-witted disciples in the Gospel of Mark, has an interesting suggestion as to why Peter should be so named. We usually take 'rock' (the meaning of the name Peter in Greek) to suggest firmness of foundation — appropriate for one on whom the Church is built — but Tolbert rather provocatively

describes the disciples as 'the rocky ground'[1] where the word is
heard with joy until difficulties arise and then the hearers fall
away.

It is against the failure of the disciples to comprehend, against
their ultimate failure to support him, that the drama of the
suffering and death of Jesus is played out. The story is told in
such a way that those listening are left in no doubt as to what
the appropriate response should be and therefore appreciate the
ever widening chasm between the 'call' of Jesus and the
'response' of the disciples — finding them sleeping is but a
metaphor for their general inability to respond. The narrator
directs the reader/listener towards that correct response by two
means: firstly an unambiguous presentation of Jesus, and
secondly by the actions or words of anonymous figures who
form a contrast with the disbelieving disciples. The Gospel
opens with almost abrupt directness: 'The beginning of the
good news of Jesus Christ, the Son of God.' (1: 1) For the
narrator, and thus the reader, Jesus is the hero of the story,
therefore any failure to respond to him is clearly marked. The
second device, the use of contrast figures, culminates in the
response of the centurion, 'Truly this man was God's Son!'
(15: 39)

If we imagine a red thread connecting these characters they
form a group embodying an alternative response and one which
is vindicated by the narrative; they also include several women.
So we have Simon's mother-in-law, whose response to her
healing is 'to serve', to minister, 'to wait on them' (1: 31) as the
angels 'waited on him' in the wilderness (1: 13); then the healed
leper, who despite the injunction to say nothing, takes it upon
himself to 'proclaim it freely' (1: 45). The man with the unclean
spirit cries out to Jesus, 'What have you to do with me, Jesus,
Son of the Most High God?' And when he is cured, he too
proclaims 'how much Jesus had done for him' (5: 7, 20). The
woman with the haemorrhage manifests courage and trust in
initiating her own cure and again proclaims publicly telling 'the
whole truth' (5: 33). The Syro-Phoenician woman confronts
Jesus directly with the limitations of his own vision in that most

extraordinary episode, 'Sir, even the dogs under the table eat the children's crumbs.'[2] (7: 24–30). The astounding honesty of the father who expresses the ambivalence of his faith, 'Lord I believe, help my unbelief!' (9: 24) rather than the naive optimism of the disciples, marks his place on this list. The blind beggar 'sees' who Jesus is, 'Jesus, Son of David, have mercy on me.'(10: 47) Finally the widow who puts in her whole living (12: 41–4) and the woman who prophetically anoints the head of Jesus (14: 3–9) demonstrate the right response, the practice of the kingdom. These are the people who make up the 'honours list' in Mark's Gospel! None of them is named, few are remembered. Yet these marginal people could be described as the true followers of Jesus, the underground movement. To this list I want to add the female slave.

Now we can return to the story, having filled out the background to Peter's behaviour and having given the maidservant a context. We can place her in the role of the other seekers for the truth, 'You also were with Jesus, the man from Nazareth.' The careful placing of her text against the text of the trial of Jesus presents us with two contrasting interrogations. On one level the might of the law is assembled: all the chief priests, the elders and the scribes and at the top of this hierarchy is the high priest who will question Jesus. Yet this court which should seek the truth is a false one. 'Now the chief priests and the whole council were looking for testimony against Jesus to put him to death; but they found none.' (14: 55) Those who should represent justice accept false testimony and when they do hear the truth they cannot recognise it and interpret it as blasphemy.

Down below in the courtyard the second 'trial' is taking place. Instead of the mighty power of patriarchal rule we see a woman who in terms of social status could not occupy a lower place. She is a female slave. She is one of the slaves of the high priest carrying out the 'show trial' above. She sees Peter, stares at him, and pronounces with conviction, 'You also were with him.' Peter denies it. It is after all his testimony against her 'worthless' one. The servant gathers her own support and says to the bystanders, 'This man is one of them.' In contrast to the conflicting

testimony in the courtroom above, here the witnesses agree and
the maidservant is supported, 'Certainly you are one of them;
for you are a Galilean.'(14: 70) For the third time Peter denies it
and then hearing the cock crow he remembers the prophecy of
Jesus, recognises his falsehood, and in the poignant words of the
Gospel, 'he broke down and wept'. The female slave has
presided over the trial of Peter, he has been found guilty, but no
condemnation or beating follows. Justice has been done, the
truth is revealed and Peter's pain is punishment enough. He
follows the other deserting disciples and disappears from the
story.

So in powerful reversal and juxtaposition of roles the high
priest and the Sanhedrin fail to judge justly and thus fail to see
the truth; and the female slave of that same high priest judges
rightly and reveals the truth. It is commonplace to contrast the
cowardice of Peter with the courage of Jesus. But we could make
another crossover between the two stories: the two who speak
the truth are Jesus and the woman. They are both confronted by
false testimony but they are not deflected from their path. The
woman takes on the prophetic role of one who persists in
naming and exposing the truth. She is as persistent as Jesus —
on whose behalf she appears to speak — 'Truly I tell you this day
you will deny me . . .' (14: 30) In remembering the fulfilment of
that prophecy we recall Peter's denial but fail to remember the
woman who confronts him, 'This man is one of them.' (14: 69)

All commentators have great difficulty with the passage,
particularly in the light of the future role of Peter, but they miss
the role of the woman. She is seen merely as an instrument to
tell Peter's story, but this changes when we begin to see the
woman not simply as 'other' to Peter but as a prophetic voice in
her own right. Does she not find her place in this Gospel of
reversals? 'But they were silent for on the way they had argued
with one another who was the greatest. He sat down and called
the twelve and said to them, "Whoever wants to be first must be
last of all and servant of all."' (9: 35)

In this case the maidservant takes on the public role of
prosecutor and serves the truth. The one from whom most was

expected — Peter as leader of the disciples — fails, and one from whom nothing is expected — a maidservant of the high priest — tenaciously persists in revealing the truth. The gentile woman who confronted Jesus was motivated by the needs of her sick child, but these women who appear and disappear in these last stages of the Gospel appear to have no ulterior motive. In the case of the woman anointing Jesus the act is initiated by the woman, it takes place in front of witnesses and is challenged by them but is named by Jesus as good. The woman is silent, she does not speak in her own defence but is defended by Jesus. In this case the woman also initiates the action, or rather the conversation. Like the Syro-Phoenician woman she persists in her questions and — uniquely — draws her own support. This is a very public act which presumably could leave her open to mockery or criticism. Reading with one eye we see the weakness of Peter exposed; opening both eyes we see the strength and courage of the maidservant. If Peter is the anti-hero and foil to the heroic fidelity of Jesus, then the woman must take her place among the unsung heroines who, despite her apparent powerlessness, names Peter and challenges him to discipleship. More than that, her accurate judgment stands out like a sharp light against the corrupt power of the Sanhedrin. Her position is affirmed and her story confirmed not by direct comment from Jesus, who is facing his own trial, but by being interpolated with that story. Framing and being framed by the story of the trial of Jesus casts light on this text. On one level the contrast is almost ludicrously uneven — Jesus faces the full force of the law and is utterly vulnerable, surrounded by hostile forces. Peter down below is questioned by an anonymous servant girl. If Peter's failure were not so tragic it would be laughable. It is also comically disproportionate — to set this woman in a parallel role to that of the high priest — but this is a Gospel of ludicrous reversals. 'But many who are first will be last and the last will be first.' (10: 31) The narrative demands to be read against the grain.

The maidservant, having fulfilled her role, disappears. So in the end must we agree that she has been used by the narrator merely as an instrument to allow the fulfilment of the prophecy? Peter too disappears from view but is mentioned again when the women at the tomb are instructed to, 'Go tell his disciples and Peter that he is going ahead of you to Galilee; there you will see him just as he told you.' (16: 7) There is some irony in the fact that Peter's last appearance in Mark's Gospel should be this encounter with the maidservant and that his knowledge of the death and resurrection of Jesus will depend on the testimony of women. In these final acts of the Gospel the only disciples who remain are the women, the named women 'who used to follow him and provided for him when he was in Galilee' and 'many other women who had come up with him to Jerusalem'(15: 41). But even these female disciples appear to desert at the very last moment. Peter left his encounter weeping; these women flee the tomb in terror and say nothing. The unfinished business and the open ending suggest this story concludes elsewhere. Confronted with the utter failure of the male disciples and the flight of the women followers, the reader could be left adrift. But then we need to recall those signals passed from hand to hand along the way, signals of an alternative response, of another possibility, signals which always came from the most unlikely of sources: from the blind, the deaf, the lepers, even a scribe (12: 34), from a woman across the boundary, and women crossing boundaries, finally from a centurion acclaiming Jesus as the Son of God, and including along the way one of the maidservants of the high priest who, perhaps unintentionally, certainly without guile, served the truth.

Chapter 8

Placing Women

One of the Pharisees asked Jesus to eat with him, and he went into the Pharisee's house and took his place at the table. And a woman in the city, who was a sinner, having learned that he was eating in the Pharisee's house, brought an alabaster jar of ointment. She stood behind him at his feet, weeping and began to bathe his feet with her tears and dry them with her hair. Then she continued kissing his feet and anointing them with the ointment. Now when the Pharisee who had invited him saw it, he said to himself, 'If this man were a prophet, he would have known who and what kind of woman this is who is touching him — that she is a sinner.' Jesus spoke up and said to him, 'Simon, I have something to say to you.' 'Teacher,' he replied, 'Speak.' 'A certain creditor had two debtors; one owed five hundred denarii and the other fifty. When they could not pay, he cancelled the debts for both of them. Now which of them will love him more?' Simon answered, 'I suppose the one for whom he cancelled the greater debt.' And Jesus said to him, 'You have judged rightly.' Then turning toward the woman he said to Simon, 'Do you see this woman? I entered your house; you gave me no water for my feet, but she has bathed my feet with her tears and dried them with her hair. You gave me no kiss, but from the time I came in she has not stopped kissing my feet. You did not anoint my head with oil, but she has anointed my feet with ointment. Therefore, I tell you, her sins which were many have been forgiven; hence she has shown great love. But the one to whom little is forgiven, loves little.' Then he said to her, 'Your sins are forgiven.' But those who were at table with him began to say among themselves, 'Who is this who even forgives sins?' And he said to the woman, 'Your faith has saved you; go in peace.' (Luke 7: 36–50)

From the outset I have to confess a great resistance to this text — or rather to the traditional readings of the text. The delight with which I encounter the stories of the woman anointing the head of Jesus in Mark and in Matthew is replaced by a sense of great unease when I read Luke's story. As I suggested when we looked at Mark's story, despite the injunction to remember that woman, the irony is that the woman remembered is the 'great sinner' from Luke although Luke's version is the only one which does not tell the story 'in memory of her'![1] The power of the narrative together with a tradition which has reinforced this perspective in practice has ensured that the memory carried is that of a great sinner forgiven by Jesus; for example, the heading to the text in three different editions of the Bible refers to 'a sinful woman forgiven'. Its effect on women is to hold them in a subservient dependent position, to keep them 'in their place'. The woman never speaks and her actions are encircled and interpreted by the two men, first Simon and then Jesus. Can this represent 'good news' for women? Or do we have to read it against its purpose? Should we read it precisely in order to resist it? In what way, if any, can this text bless us?

The story is set in the framework of a comparison between the practices of Jesus and of John the Baptist. The more ascetic practices of John are contrasted with the eating and drinking of the 'Son of Man', 'Look, a glutton and a drunkard, a friend of tax-collectors and sinners! Nevertheless wisdom is justified by her children.' (Luke 7: 35)

Immediately there follows the story of the invitation from the Pharisee to Jesus to dine with him. This is not the first time such a criticism is directed at Jesus and followed by a table-setting. The first time the comment about eating and drinking with tax-collectors and sinners was made was in the context of the great banquet hosted by Levi at which 'there was a large crowd of tax-collectors and others' (5: 29). A pattern is established whereby the saying is followed by an illustration. It happens again in Luke 15 at the introduction to the parables of the lost sheep culminating in the parable of the Prodigal Son. So we expect this story to fill out in narrative form the response of Jesus to his critics.

No time is wasted before the main characters are introduced

and juxtaposed. In fact we could speak of two triangular relationships: we have the woman and the Pharisee in relation to Jesus; then we have Jesus and the Pharisee in relation to the woman. The Pharisee hosts the meal, he invites Jesus to dine and Jesus enters and takes his place at the table. Then the woman is introduced — as a sinner. The polarisation is clear: the Pharisees have already been introduced as those who, in refusing the baptism of John, 'rejected God's purpose for themselves' (7: 30). The woman, on the other hand, is labelled as a 'sinner', which in this context can be translated as 'friend of Jesus' (7: 33). This perspective is supported by her actions which are not hidden but in the context rather bold; having learned that Jesus is dining in this house, she arrives with her alabaster jar of ointment. Her action is clearly premeditated. She stands behind Jesus weeping and then proceeds to bathe his feet, dry them and anoint them. As if this were not enough, she continues kissing and anointing the feet in a demonstrably extravagant manner.

It seems to me that attempts to deny the obvious eroticism are misplaced. The gestures are so clearly sensual and intimate and take place during a banquet, the implication must be that the woman is a prostitute — although Luke does not describe her as such.[2] The whole drama of the story derives from such an insinuation — thus Simon, 'If this man were a prophet he would have known who and what kind of a woman this is who is touching him — that she is a sinner.' (7: 39) Luke's usual ironic devices come into play; it is not the knowledge of Jesus which is deficient but that of Simon, the Pharisee, who — understandably in the context — judges the woman on the basis of expectation and experience. Women like her, according to his categories, are sinners. Jesus, who is indeed a prophet, sees beyond the obvious and redefines the woman. The parable of the two debtors is clear and Simon answers correctly that the one who owed more will 'love him more'. However then Jesus turns towards the woman and addresses Simon with a compelling phrase: 'Do you see this woman?' (7: 44) Up to this point in the story we have seen the woman through the eyes of Simon and following the lead of the narrator we too have defined her as a prostitute and drawn certain conclusions from that. Now, like Simon, we are asked to look again, 'Do you see this woman?' Jesus then describes the actions of the woman according to a very different frame of reference, that of appropriate hospitality. The tables turn as the woman and Simon are juxtaposed and reappear in an unexpected configuration: you gave me no water, she has bathed my feet; you gave me no kiss, she has not stopped kissing me; you gave me no oil, she has anointed my feet. The roles are reversed; the text is subverted here from within by Jesus! The one defined as a sinner is redescribed as 'the woman who loved much', one who provided all the courtesies which would be expected of a good host; meanwhile the one described as host is redefined as one who has fallen short of his duties, 'a sinner'. 'Do you see this woman?' Like Simon, the reader also feels that she has been set up! The narrator has led us carefully towards one particular reading of the woman as prostitute, only to pull away this definition from before our eyes and turn us around, convert us, invite us to look again, 'Do you see this woman?' Then almost as an afterthought Jesus adds, 'Her sins which were many, have been forgiven; hence she has shown great love.' (7: 47) The implication here is that the woman was already forgiven and the great love shown is a consequence, not a cause of that forgiveness. As the woman leaves, Jesus addresses her with the same words that he uses to the woman with the haemorrhage (8: 48), 'Your faith has saved you, go in peace.' (7: 50)

So one woman, two stories: the woman seen by Simon and the guests at the table — the woman as sinner, as prostitute; and the woman seen by Jesus as one 'who has shown great love'. The tradition seems to have been more comfortable with the notion of the great sinner forgiven by Jesus than the great lover praised by Jesus! Do we solve our difficulties with the story by recasting it in the framework proposed by Barbara Reid who sees the woman as a disciple who prefigures the Christ, 'I am among you as one who serves.'[3] On one level this seems appropriate. The woman's great love and act of service is honoured. On the other hand such self-effacing gestures on the part of women have led to the invisibility of the ministry of women. The admonition to the disciples to serve one another comes in the context of a dispute among the male disciples as to which of them is the greatest (22: 24–7). It is powerful precisely because it is counter-cultural. In a similar way when Jesus chooses to wash the feet of the disciples as narrated in the Gospel of John, its power comes from the element of surprise, from the reversal of roles. There is a danger in applying the same demands to women in a way which reinforces the traditional expectations of what women's tasks are. One is particularly wary of this when reading the Gospel of Luke because we see no evidence for the genuine discipleship of women. This particular story is followed by a description of Jesus going with the twelve through the cities accompanied by a group of women 'who provided for them out of their resources'(8: 3). The women are not described as disciples but, in now time-worn fashion, are there to support the ministry of men.

In Luke's story the prophet is clearly Jesus; the woman has no prophetic role. She does not anoint the head, but the feet. There is no suggestion that she anticipates his burial. And there is no dispute about waste. In that sense we can agree that Luke is telling a very different story which happens to have some of the same elements as that told by Mark, Matthew and John, but is in effect a quite different tale. Her story, inasmuch as we can describe it as 'her' story, does not flow into the larger narrative as those other stories do. So how should we read it?

As I have indicated, I feel that we run into problems when we describe the woman either as a 'great sinner' or as a 'great lover'. We continue to operate with an unhealthy and unhelpful polarisation of women into two stereotypical positions: the whore and the virgin, the bad woman and the good woman. Rescuing the fallen woman and placing her on a pedestal still leaves her in a very precarious position — pedestals are notoriously uncomfortable! So let us abandon both saint and sinner and revisit the story.

One way of doing this is to recognise that this text is not really about the woman at all! It is not 'her' story and it is not told in her memory. Paradoxically by de-centring her we may find her appropriate place. I suggest that we read this piece as a parabolic narrative, an enacted parable.[4] In fact we could see some parallels between the equally unaptly named parable of the 'Prodigal Son' and this story of the 'Forgiven Sinner'. In both cases the focus of attention on a single character tends to inhibit response to the dynamics of the narrative as a whole. In the case of the Prodigal Son the attention focused on the younger son misses the point of the inability of the elder son to join the feast and begs the question, 'Who is really lost here?' In our narrative the attention we focus on the woman fails to address adequately the response of Simon, the Pharisee. In both cases the texts follow criticism of Jesus for welcoming sinners and eating with them (7: 33; 15: 2). The audiences in the two instances are made up of the two opposed groups, tax-collectors and sinners on the one hand, scribes and Pharisees on the other. In the first story the meal with the Pharisee is interrupted by the 'sinner' in order to test the issue of 'dining with sinners' or, to put it in broader terms, in order to test the issue of boundaries. In the parable of the Prodigal Son, the feast for the younger son is interrupted by the elder in order to test the same issue of outsiders and insiders.

Let us return to focus on our text. We have now recast it as a parabolic narrative which frames an actual parable, that of the two debtors. It is clearly a set piece where the players are ciphers in a story which has a much broader focus than the forgiveness of the sins of an unnamed woman. In Luke's Gospel there is an extraordinary amount of wining and dining! The table is the place where issues are debated with disciples and followers, at Bethsaida, the Passover meal and Emmaus, for example; with tax-collectors like Levi and Zaccheus, and no less than three times with Pharisees. This is the first of these meals. At this stage in his ministry the Pharisees are interested in Jesus — we are told that they came from every village to hear him (5: 17) — and he has the advantage of being the only character who can freely move between the two juxtaposed groups, tax-collectors and sinners, scribes and Pharisees. Meals with Jesus become places where issues under dispute are tested. For example, the next meal taken with a Pharisee deals with the issue of purity (11: 37–53).

This first meal deals with the more fundamental question about how Jesus is perceived. The people, having witnessed the raising of the widow's son at Nain, had acclaimed him a prophet, 'A great prophet has risen among us! God has looked favourably upon his people.' (7: 16) It is this word about Jesus which has been spreading about Judea which will be tested in the house of Simon. It is not simply whether Jesus is a prophet, but the whole understanding of prophecy which is at stake here.

The religious and social code of the Pharisees works on a system of clear boundaries, carefully delineated: space and time are marked out. Anyone who crosses or blurs those boundaries is perceived as a threat. With this understanding we can begin to see how the practices of Jesus are highly destabilising for that closed order. We can then observe the pattern of the story as an illustration of this subversive or destabilising practice of Jesus and begin to appreciate why ultimately the Pharisees bar Jesus from their houses and why the chief priests and the scribes look for a way to be rid of him. The Pharisee invites Jesus to dine and we are told that Jesus entered the house and took his place at the table. The Pharisee at this stage is in control: it is his house, his space, and Jesus is seated at his table as his guest. The roles are clear and by rights the Pharisee as host can determine the course of action. Then a woman, a sinner, enters. Immediately the situation changes and the atmosphere is charged with tension. The world of the outside — of sinners, of the impure — has entered the house. The two worlds are crossing over in and through the person of Jesus. With what group will he ally himself? In order to maintain the distinctions, Jesus must make the boundaries clear, he must mark his card and the Pharisee can breathe freely again. The woman touches Jesus, not surreptitiously, but with deliberately provocative gestures. 'Then she continued kissing his feet and anointing them with the ointment.' (7: 38) There is no ambiguity here, at least not for the Pharisee. The case is clear-cut. 'If this man were a prophet, he would have known who and what kind of woman this is, who is touching him —that she is a sinner.' (7: 39) This is the issue upon which the story turns. Instead of responding directly to the unvoiced but perceived criticism, Jesus teases Simon with an apparently obvious parable about two debtors. Simon, having given the correct reply, is trapped as he watches while the parable is applied to his own situation. He had expected the prophetic skills of Jesus to be used in revealing and condemning the sinfulness of the woman; instead, the discerning eye of the prophet has read his thoughts and judged his actions. The meaning of prophecy has been subverted and 'the limitations of the Pharisee's understanding are blatantly exposed'.[5] In a complete reversal of roles the 'righteous' Pharisee finds himself in the place of the 'sinner', the one who has 'fallen short' of the required duties; and the one named as sinner has taken the position of the 'righteous one', having demonstrated hospitality to Jesus and more importantly receptivity to his word, to his teaching. The social and religious world of the Pharisee has been invaded. Not only has Jesus refused to recognise the existing boundaries, he has radically redrawn the map so that by the end of the story we no longer recognise 'the house of the Pharisee' but instead see a space dominated by Jesus where having received the woman he can now dismiss her, 'Go in peace.'

The story turns on the dialogue with Simon, on the conversation which overturns the definitions of 'sinner' and of 'prophet'. The earlier meal of Jesus with Levi, the tax-collector, had taken place within the house of Levi with a large number of tax-collectors present. This was criticised by the Pharisees but was not nearly as threatening or offensive as this invasion of their space by Jesus who virtually takes over the house and table and receives a 'sinner' as guest. The crossing of boundaries represents the breaking down of the purity code, the breaking down of a social order which has operated according to the principle of religious and social elitism.

What is finally shocking to the Pharisee is not the presence of the woman or even her actions — this is only what one would expect of such a woman — but the re-interpretation of those actions, the re-ordering of the system, the re-vising of religious categories, the re-naming by Jesus and the final reversal of roles. It is as radical as the reversal implied at the Passover meal when

Jesus defines himself as 'one who serves'. But in this case the point is not that the woman serves Jesus but that Jesus, in receiving her service, takes it up and casts it in a totally new mould. It is no longer the expected behaviour of a prostitute but the action of a generous host, the action of one open and hospitable to the Word. It is love, not law, which determines who shall sit at this table, which is no longer the table of Simon the Pharisee but a banquet hosted by Jesus which has been shockingly, disturbingly extended to include the woman. The prophet is not the one who maintains the status quo — as implied by the comment of Simon — but the one who breaks the mould, so that the last will be first.

Shifting the focus from the woman as repentant sinner has enabled us to see a much more radical agenda at work. The concern of the narrator is to mark Jesus as prophet who will not simply dine with 'tax-collectors and sinners' but will dine with Pharisees precisely in order to move into the very heart of the religious system and expose it as a system of oppression.

The tragedy for women reading this story is that the woman used as an instrument for radical reform in this text is not, like Levi, invited to discipleship but disappears possibly under the cover of 'some women who had been cured of evil spirits and infirmities; Mary called Magdalene, from whom seven demons had gone out and Joanna the wife of Herod's steward Chuza, and Susanna, and many others who provided for them out of their resources'(8: 2). But even if we do imagine her as part of this group, there is no textual link to connect her with Mary Magdalene, and such a link has resulted in an unfortunate distortion of that tradition.

In a paradoxical way decentring the woman, downplaying her importance as repentant sinner, frees her to return to a more interesting role in the story. Freed from the dual burdens which 'great sin' or 'great love' impose, we can see the woman as the catalyst for the shattering of boundaries. Simon the Pharisee attempted to 'place' Jesus and to put the woman 'in her place', but it is he who is displaced. Like women before her and women who have come after her, her role on the threshold between the old and the new is critical. Such liminal characters become symbols for the crossing over represented by the prophet Jesus. They should not be domesticated or controlled by a pious moralising of their stories.

DISPLACING WOMEN

Along the Margins and in the Gaps

Chapter 9

Missing Women

Now the tax-collectors and sinners were coming near to listen to him. And the Pharisees and the scribes were grumbling and saying, 'This fellow welcomes sinners and eats with them.'
So he told them this parable: which one of you having a hundred sheep . . ?
Or what woman having ten silver coins . . ?
Then Jesus said, 'There was a man who had two sons . . . But we had to celebrate and rejoice because this brother of yours was dead and has come to life; he was lost and has been found.'
(Luke 15: 1–32)

These stories are so familiar that the recitation of even one phrase is sufficient to send the whole story flooding back to us. There are strong images helped by countless illustrations of shepherds carrying lambs and fathers welcoming home their long lost sons. Less frequent are the pictures of women searching for lost coins, less strong is the picture of the woman hosting a party. In fact in my experience if you ask a group whether there is any incident in scripture which describes a woman hosting a feast, this parable does not spring instantly to mind. Only by prompting is it recalled even among a scripturally literate group. The woman like the coin has been lost to our collective, our communal memory. It does not have the same powerful effect as the stories which shape our consciousness. Such stories are as familiar as the story which follows the question asked at Passover, 'Why is this night different from all other nights?', or the story which begins, 'On the night before he was betrayed . . .'

We know these stories by heart. That is to say the knowledge is felt, it is embodied, it flows in us and through us. It flows out from us into actions which shape our lives. The stories we tell inform us and by constant repetition form us. The process eventually becomes unconscious.

It is not sufficient simply to retrieve lost texts about women and highlight them, although that is vitally important, but it is even more important to release these texts into the flow of stories which are ritually represented to us, which become part of that common memory. The stories then take their place in the process of healing the imagination so that we can know them by heart. 'Shaping and reshaping the imagination is one of the central functions of the public reading of scripture as sacred story . . . As stories about God and us, they shape our images of reality, of life and of ourselves.'[1]

These three parables are stories about God. The description of the third parable as the story of the Prodigal Son has dominated the interpretation of the preceding shorter stories. They have been misrepresented as stories about repentant sinners, but as someone pointed out, sheep and coins don't repent! They have also been misrepresented as stories about the need for the individual sinner to make his/her peace with God. (In this context it is of course worth noting that there is no female sinner but there is a female seeker.) The repentant sinner is not the primary focus of the parables. These parables are told in a community context: tax-collectors and sinners are drawing near, Pharisees and scribes are grumbling. These are the groups to whom the stories are directed. They are stories about inclusion and exclusion. They are parables which break down the traditional boundaries and draw up new lines. They are stories about the pull towards and away from the unrestricted communion offered by God as God's gift.

These three stories are parables about God. They shatter the image of God. They subvert the traditional understanding of God as tribal, of God as male, of God as patriarch. They are told in the context of a complaint from the Pharisees, 'This fellow welcomes sinners and eats with them.' This is not the first and neither will it be the last time that they make such a complaint, and to put it into perspective, and to demonstrate just how seriously they regarded such breaches of 'etiquette', one commentator has suggested that Jesus was crucified because of the 'way he ate'. I think we can take it that this is a reference to the company Jesus keeps at table rather than his table manners!

(Although that was also the subject of criticism, 'The Pharisee was amazed to see that he did not first wash before dinner.' (11.38)) The table becomes the focus for complaints about the lifestyle of Jesus. The table becomes the primary symbol of the praxis of Jesus. So such a criticism is serious, it is tantamount to naming Jesus as subversive. So how does he respond to such a serious charge? He doesn't take his critics head on and confront them with counter-accusations as he has done before, 'Woe to you Pharisees, you love the best seats in the synagogue . . .' Instead he tells them some stories, stories which attempt to create a different space in which it might be possible to imagine differently. The stories shape a different vision of relationships within the community, of relationships with God.

Instead of highlighting the parable about the woman seeking the coin, this time I want to start with the third parable focusing on the image of God and then look again at the first two parables in that light. My reason for this is my fear of isolating the second parable, bracketing it as the 'female interest story', the crumb which falls from the rich table of the third story. This is somewhat analogous to the attempt to redress patriachal imagery for God by speaking about the Spirit as the feminine aspect of the divine.[2] We are still left with two clear masculine images and a vague third (a vague bird!). So here we have two apparently strong images, shepherd and father, and the weaker third character. A shift in focus may help. In the third parable we are missing women but we are seeking God. As assiduously as the woman searching for the lost coin, we need to search this story for an understanding of God. (Even this is a distortion because the real focus is God seeking us!) If women can find themselves in relation to God only in stories about women, then that relationship is seriously impoverished. Feminist readings cannot concern themselves only with texts about women, for not only would the repertoire be seriously limited, but such selective reading would reinscribe sexism. It would suggest that stories about women remain in those brackets — stories about women — instead of stories which concern the whole community. For this reason throughout these essays I have attempted to release such stories into the flow of the whole narrative.

These are God-seeking parables. They cast light on one another. But instead of reading them as building to the climax of the third, we are going to read them backwards allowing the third to illuminate, and then in turn to be illuminated by, the other two.

'There was a man who had two sons': little wonder that the elder feels aggrieved. No one ever refers to this as the parable of the elder son! Yet if we recall the context we remember that there are two groups listening to the parables — tax-collectors and sinners, scribes and Pharisees. The story is addressed to both. By attending to the role of the father we can keep that focus. When the younger son leaves and travels to a distant country he is separating himself from his roots. When he goes to work as a swineherd for the despised other, the gentile, he alienates himself not just from his family but from his religious roots. This is indeed a distant place. As far as his community is concerned it is tantamount to his having died. It is worse than that, his name would probably never be spoken again. In order to appreciate the enormity of what occurs in the second stage of the story — the reception by the father — we need to visualise what the son has done. This is the reverse of the usual order where the preacher focuses on the great sin of the son and therefore on his repentance followed by his forgiveness. But this is an example of *felix culpa*, that extraordinary idea of a happy fault. A great sin, one which in this community would mean a permanent state of ostracism, needs to be highlighted so that even greater grace may be demonstrated.

If we read with the focus on the father, that shift from sin to grace is clear. We hear the son rehearsing an appropriate penitential speech, 'I will get up and go to my father and I will say to him, "Father I have sinned against heaven and before you; I am no longer worthy to be called your son; treat me as one of your hired hands."' So he sets off. So far he is working from the same script as our traditional preacher, 'Acknowledge your fault, confess your sin and Almighty God will forgive you.' But that is not the script of the parable! A different agenda is being set: 'But while he was still far off, his father saw him and was filled with compassion; he ran and put his arms around him and kissed him.' These are the central lines of the story. This is the pivot on which the story turns, the point at which the traditional reading is overturned, subverted, transformed. Remember that we as readers have been privy to the son's expression of repentance. We have overheard him rehearsing his speech, but at this point the father has heard nothing. He does not wait for any words but offers his unconditional love. Grace is not earned. Grace pours out. Let us look at what happens in detail. 'While he was still far off, his father saw him . . .' The son is still 'distant' but the father has him in his sight. Then comes the critical phrase '[he] was filled with compassion'. We need to examine that word *compassion*, literally 'to suffer with'. It has tended in recent times to be used as a 'soft touch' word. It is nothing of the sort. The original Greek word means something like 'wrenching your guts, tearing your heart'. It is a powerful word, a word which can raise the dead to life. So it shouldn't be tossed about as if it were a soft liberal option, a nice word. It is not nice, it is awesome. It turns the thought to deed! It is not simply a feeling, it is a praxis. It is the praxis of Jesus. In Hebrew the word 'compassion' has its root in the word for womb. So to speak of the God of compassion is to speak of a God who bears life, who nurtures life, a God of womb-like love. The father in the parable reminds us of the words of the Lord in Jeremiah (31: 20):

Is Ephraim my dear son?
Is he the child I delight in?
As often as I speak against him,
I still remember him.
Therefore I am deeply moved for him.

This is a weak translation. The text suggests a 'yearning' which is the word used in the Jerusalem Bible and Marcus Borg goes further and for the last two lines suggests:

Therefore my womb trembles for him;
I will truly show motherly compassion upon him.[3]

Borg extends the phrase 'filled with compassion' to suggest its rich meaning, its rich sources in the tradition. The yearning and longing for his child impels the father to action. He ran and put his arms around him (literally, 'fell on his neck') and kissed him. Several commentators point out that it is quite ludicrous for such a figure to run. It is inappropriate behaviour. It would have caused a reaction of shock in the listeners. So what is going on here? The script of what God is like is being rewritten. The image of God as patriarchal father is being overthrown. The image of God as judge, justly punishing the wicked and rewarding the just, is replaced by a model of God as one who yearns for and seeks out the lost, one who is filled with tender compassion, one who even before the words of repentance are uttered offers unconditional love. We listen to the son attempt to make his prepared speech, but the first words are barely out of his mouth when the speech is interrupted and left unfinished as the father calls out, 'Let us eat and celebrate.' There is a deep irony when we examine the missing words which should follow 'I am no longer worthy to be called your son.' They refer of course to the suggestion, 'treat me as one of your hired hands'. Once again the reader is privy to this, but according to our narrative the father does not wait for this suggestion to be voiced in his presence but interrupts the penitential psalm with his own suggestion which utterly transcends what the son had in mind and transforms his condition from penitent slave to favoured guest: 'Quickly bring out a robe — the best one — and put it on him; put a ring on his finger and sandals on his feet. And get the fatted calf and kill it . . .' This is not about repentance followed by forgiveness. If anything it is the other way around, '. . . God's forgiving love, not human evil determines God's relationship with humanity.'[4] It is indeed about *felix culpa*, 'happy fault' and oh such happy grace! It is about the unmerited unconditional offer of love.

It is love which creates the possibility for repentance, for true *metanoia*, 'change of heart'. Conversion is not a condition but a consequence of God's love.[5] Once again, here, as in the house of Simon the Pharisee, love, not the law, transforms relationships.

The parable does not end here. There are two groups listening to this story. The elder son is angry, he refuses to join the party. The father hearing that he has refused to come in goes out, like the shepherd seeking the missing sheep, and entreats him. But the son answers, 'Listen! For all these years I have been working like a slave for you . . .' This is of course ironic: the elder son sees himself as a slave; the younger son had intended to return as 'a hired servant'. Both have missed the mark of the relationship which is on offer. The father redefines it for both of them. The language of servant and master, the relationships of the patriarchal household have been replaced with the offer of unconditional love, 'all that is mine is yours'. Such love carries obligations which transcend duty and law, 'But we had to celebrate . . .', literally, 'it was necessary to celebrate'. The elder son can be sought out but he is not compelled to come in; he stands not under the law but under the invitation of grace.

Patriarchy has been radically subverted. The elder son expresses the disorientation of those listening, 'This fellow welcomes sinners and eats with them.' 'But when this son of yours came back, who had devoured your property with prostitutes, you killed the fatted calf for him.' It makes no sense according to this scheme. The reorientation depends on the willingness of those listening to accept the call out of servility into freedom, to learn the grammar of love and the politics of compassion.[6]

Now we can look back, reeling perhaps from the shock of a disturbing model of God, to the images in the first two parables. These are surely safe and tame: a shepherd carrying a lost lamb, a woman sweeping out her house. I think these pieces need to be read with an awareness of the foolishness of God which was demonstrated in the parable of the prodigal father. It made no sense to offer such an extravagant feast to the wayward son. He did not deserve it.

So with some tentativeness we read, 'Which one of you having a hundred sheep and losing one, does not leave the ninety-nine in the wilderness . . ?' Rhetorical questions usually demand an affirmative answer but the answer here is surely negative. No one — in their right mind — would leave ninety-nine sheep to go after one! This is a parable, not a moral tale. It works by the process of disorienting and reorienting, by the juxtaposition of the ordinary with the extraordinary. Luke's irony is clearly at work.

The ordinary shepherd does this crazy thing and then invites his friends and neighbours for a feast, 'Rejoice with me . . .' So even in this parable we have an image of a God whose love transcends the bounds of logic. But what of the figure of the shepherd imaging God? Again we must attend to the groups to whom the parables are addressed: tax-collectors and sinners on the one hand, scribes and Pharisees on the other. The tax-collectors and sinners are comforted by these stories — they who are traditionally excluded and despised are brought in. But what of the religious leaders? They will certainly feel unhappy with the process of welcome and the offer of feasting to sinners who have not yet made restitution. They will feel uneasy at the emphasis on seeking out the lost, conscious that this criticism is directed at them. They will be shocked to be asked as religious leaders to think of themselves as shepherds, and even more disturbed when they realise that the despised shepherd images God.[7] The scribes and Pharisees will hear the echo of the prophet Ezekiel (34: 4, 6, 15), 'You have not strengthened the weak, you have not healed the sick . . . my sheep were scattered with no one to search or seek for them. . . . I myself will be the shepherd of my sheep . . . I will seek the lost and I will bring back the strayed.'

So within that apparently gentle model of the shepherd searching out the lost one we have both a rebuke and an invitation, 'he calls together his friends and neighbours, saying to them "Rejoice with me . . ."' The final image with which the listeners are left is not of punishment or chastisement but of feasting and celebration.

If we follow the topsy-turvy logic of the foolishness of God as illustrated in the framing parables, what do we say about the

woman searching for the lost coin? It is difficult to get excited
about the search for a coin. There is no plaintive crying as from
the lost lamb; there is no embracing and kissing as with a lost
child; there is no pull at the heart-strings of our emotions. In
fact it seems sensible to search for a lost coin, particularly if it is
worth a day's wages. But then we realise that this woman is fairly
wealthy. This is not her only coin and she is not described as a
'poor widow', for example. All of this is both refreshing and
interesting. It inhibits the rush to stereotype the woman as a
weak female, as a victim of some oppressive system. This woman
is clearly a householder. It is she who has charge of the finances.
When something is missing it is her responsibility to see it
restored. The woman cannot be faulted, she lights a lamp,
sweeps the house, searches carefully until she finds what is
missing. She is the subject of the story and exercises authority.
When she has found the coin she calls together her women
friends and neighbours, 'Rejoice with me for I have found the
coin that I had lost.' This is perhaps the only hint of foolishness:
to spend all day searching for a lost coin and then to blow it all
on a party! Is this perhaps the focus of the story? How can we
make sense of the final line, 'Just so, I tell you there is joy in the
presence of the angels of God over one sinner who repents.'
There was no sinner to repent! However there was joy and there
was a woman seeking the lost. The word used for seeking is the
same verb used by Luke in the story of Zaccheus, 'The Son of
Man has come to seek out and to save the lost.' (19: 10) In that
story too Jesus is criticised for being the guest of 'one who is a
sinner'.

So having been led in gently to this parable about a woman
searching for a coin, we are disoriented by the final image: the
rejoicing household becomes an image for the reign of God and
so the woman diligently searching portrays God, who even
when there is no urgency, goes out of her way to seek out the
lost. The woman hosts the feast with the prodigal generosity of
God. The fact that these friends and neighbours are all female
gives us our first illustration of a celebration of women church!

The idea of a woman hosting the feast, which suggests the

eschatological banquet, prepares the way for the final subversion of the patriarchal model of God which we have described in the third parable.

Feminist scripture scholar Sandra Schneiders convincingly makes the point that if Jesus had been a woman there would have been nothing revelatory about his life. As a male he challenges patriarchy effectively.[8] Elizabeth Johnson puts it even more succinctly. 'If in a patriarchal culture a woman had preached compassionate love and enacted a style of authority that serves, she would most certainly have been greeted with a colossal shrug.'[9]

Thus it was more effective to depict a patriarchal household and within that context to critique patriarchy. It was also more effective to depict a woman as a householder who by her diligent actions would have commanded respect, and then to surprise the listeners with the comparison of her feast with the heavenly banquet. Throughout all three parables the image of God is subverted and transformed by women and men for men and women. Throughout all three parables the listeners are disoriented as the model of God breaks loose from the fetters of patriarchy and is reshaped by the stories of foolish shepherds, compassionate fathers and wise women. The judgment of the scribes and Pharisees on the one who 'welcomes sinners and eats with them' is challenged by the invitations to join the feast, 'Rejoice with me.' Closed minds are opened, limited imaginations are stretched, by parables which invite us to see differently. As women reading these stories against the grain of centuries of male-centred interpretation we too continue the work of lighting lamps, sweeping out the houses and searching diligently until Wisdom's banquet is prepared for all the absent mothers, missing daughters and sisters together with the sons and brothers and fathers. The offer of grace to the originally excluded does not diminish the offer of the grace to those already present, 'All that is mine is yours.' The elder son who grumbles at the party for the returned brother or at the idea of a woman hosting the feast is not excluded but is entreated, 'Come rejoice with us!'

Chapter 10

Concealing Women

He told them another parable: 'The kingdom of heaven is like yeast that a woman took and mixed in with three measures of flour until all of it was leavened.' (Matt. 13: 33)

And again he said, 'To what shall I compare the kingdom of God? It is like yeast that a woman took and mixed in with three measures of flour until all of it was leavened.' (Luke 13: 20)

In Matthew's gospel this two line text is one of a pair in a long list of parables. In Luke, it is one of a pair inserted into a different setting. In both cases the meaning seems so obvious as not to need much elucidation: like its partner, the parable of the mustard seed, it apparently suggests that from small beginnings, seeds and yeast, great things can grow. So it tends to be passed over. Thus when the spotlight catches it, we are caught off guard. It is as if a minor character has accidentally been brought into focus. She blinks in the unaccustomed brightness and we are mildly embarrassed waiting for the moment to pass.

The story, if one can call it that, does not have the development of the opening parable in Matthew's collection of the sower with his seed falling on different kinds of ground. The woman mixing yeast with flour is every woman who has ever mixed a batch of dough and fed her family. Baking and milling were two of the domestic responsibilities of women.[1] This is a woman carrying out a traditional role or so it seems — no mystery or surprise here, nothing hidden that will not immediately be revealed.

The word parable comes from the Greek *para* meaning 'alongside' and *ballein* meaning 'to throw'. Parables tease the listener by juxtaposing the ordinary and expected with the unfamiliar. Somehow we have lost that moment of surprise in a parable which we have traditionally read as self-evident. Parables are not to be flattened into neat moral maxims or domesticated even when they refer to women!

I have spoken of *the* parable. But we have two versions, that of
Luke and that of Matthew. In order to understand the parable
fully we need to look at each text in its context. Because we are
dealing with such a short text here it is particularly illuminating
to become aware of the significance of the setting.

Matthew's parable of the leaven is one of a set in a 'day of
parables'. It marks a break between those parables told to the
crowd and those told 'in the house' to the disciples. With the
exception of the first parable of the sower all begin with the
phrase, 'The kingdom of heaven is like . . .' It is probably useful
to consider translating *basileia* as 'reign' rather than 'kingdom'.[2]
This renders us less likely to think of 'kingdom' as a place where
God rules as monarch and instead opens up a more fluid sense
of relationship with God.

Matthew's community is preoccupied with the acceptance or
rejection of the teaching of Jesus. So we have the story of the
seed falling on rocky ground and then on good soil. This is
followed by the parable of the wheat and the weeds. It seems
significant that whereas these first two parables suggest a
division between those who 'see and understand' and those
whose hearts are hardened, the pair of parables, of which our
one is the second, appears to be concerned with what God's
reign is like. It seems to me too simplistic to interpret these
parables as illustrations of 'small beginnings and great results'.
The parable of the wheat and the weeds prepares the ground for
what is surprising about God's reign. Although there is a time of
judgment, a time of harvest, for the present the wheat and the
weeds grow together. There is no premature division of the pure
and impure. So in the parable of the mustard seed, whereas we
do have a reference to the smallest seed and the greatest shrub,
we also have the description of the birds of the air coming to
nest in its branches. The possible sectarian reading of the first
parables is counteracted by the image of God's reign as
hospitable to all the birds of the air without distinction.

So we come to the parable of the leaven or the yeast. The first
shock to the listeners will be the link between leaven and God's
reign. Leaven or yeast is traditionally associated with a

corrupting force, 'Watch out and beware of the yeast of the Pharisees and the Saduccees.' (Matt. 16: 6) Once again I suggest that we do not opt for the simple interpretation i.e. that yeast is used in this case in a positive sense. If we remember the teasing nature of the parable form, it makes more sense to allow that startling juxtaposition of the positive and negative images of yeast as that which corrupts but at the same time transforms the dough. It is worth recalling that the process of bread-baking would have involved using 'sourdough' as a starter. The already fermented dough when mixed in with flour enables the whole dough to rise. The cookery writer Elizabeth David, discussing the origins of yeast bread, points out that 'eventually someone must have realised that bread made from such dough although it may have been thought to have been spoiled rose better.' However she also refers to 'the curiously ambivalent attitude towards leavened bread and leaven generally as expressed in both the Old Testament and the New, "a symbol of silent pervasive influence, usually of that which is corrupt"'.[3] The ferment indicated decay and corruption and thus was suspect. It was important, then as now, to use this 'starter' dough at precisely the right moment. If left too long it would be unfit to use and would have to be abandoned. Such yeast would indeed destroy the whole loaf. So if we allow the image to stand we have the same kind of paradox as already exists in the grinding down of corn to produce a life-sustaining food. So the dough is corrupted by the yeast but that corruption transforms the whole process. The dough rises, doubles in size and produces a large loaf.

As the listeners make the adjustment from the notion of leaven or yeast as something negative to something positive they are being converted to a new way of understanding God's reign. God's reign is not as they have imagined. This can be described as the first 'scandal' of the parable: the transference of this image of corruption into something positive and life-giving. It has the same kind of shock-effect as calling that Samaritan good!

The second element we notice is the fact that the woman is described as hiding the yeast. Unfortunately the NRSV renders the original Greek *enekrypsen* as 'mixed' rather than 'hidden'.

The idea of hiding needs to be retained in order to demonstrate that this woman in the act of concealing the yeast in the dough paradoxically reveals the reign of God. Earlier Jesus had told his disciples, 'To you it has been given to know the secrets of the kingdom of heaven' (Matt. 13: 11), and again 'I will open my mouth in parables; I will proclaim what has been hidden from the foundation of the world.' (Matt. 13: 34) Later in another parable the kingdom is decribed as 'like a treasure hidden in a field' (Matt.13: 44). It is not immediately obvious, but like the seed buried in the ground which will eventually become a tree, the yeast hidden in the dough will leaven the whole dough.

If we read the two parables of the mustard seed and the leaven as a pair, then we may feel that there is not really a very strong parallel between the great tree which emerges from the seed and the loaf of bread which results from the dough. However we need to look more closely at the amount of flour which is leavened. Our text tells us that the woman uses 'three measures of flour'. Commentators alert us to the fact that such an amount would feed one hundred people.[4] Yet this is clearly a domestic setting. So what is going on? Some listeners will hear the echo of the Genesis story (18: 1–21) where Sarah and Abraham are surprised by heavenly vistors and Sarah rushes away and takes 'three measures of flour' to make cakes. A little water and a little bread quickly translates into a feast befitting the angelic visitors. The kingdom of heaven demands a heavenly banquet, an outpouring of hospitality which presumably will feed the people of the earth as the tree offered shelter to the birds of the air. So it seems appropriate to name the woman as 'bakerwoman God' feeding her people. A woman, some leaven, three measures of flour — simple ingredients, brought together in a parable which teases us into a new understanding of God's reign.

What is most surprising then is how easily this parable has been passed over. Its meaning is apparently so transparent: 'The size of the three measures is not significant. The contrast between small beginnings and powerful influence is, as in the previous parable, obvious.'[5]

Is this, I wonder, an example of gender rendering the action insignificant? The woman, after all, was only doing what women do, baking bread for the household — a little domestic tale demonstrating, as other commentators like to point out, that God can be seen in the ordinary everyday things. It becomes suitable then for the kind of pious preaching which would extol attention to the smallest of our tasks so that the kingdom might be built up. All very admirable but, I would argue, totally missing the subversive nature of this parable. It is a parable. It demands that we tease out the meaning which is hidden like the leaven in the dough. God's reign is surprising, shocking, disturbing, scandalous. Susan Praeder, reminding us that Matthew and Luke portray Jesus as bold in his practice and proclamation of the kingdom, offers this more daring interpretation: 'Leavening is a process including leaven and wheat flour and "corrupting" wheat flour into wholly leavened wheat flour. Similarly, the kingdom involves a leavening process of sorts, a "corrupting" of the people of God through the inclusion of outcasts or the subversive transformation of the world.'[6]

So this is not a parable to be quickly glossed over, coming as it does in Matthew, in the middle of a day of parables; rather it, like each of the others, in turn, must cause us to pause and consider what sort of reign of God Jesus proclaims. God's reign appears where it is least expected and through those considered 'the least of these' like this bakerwoman. We have watched here the turning of a symbol as the leaven of the Pharisees becomes the leaven of the woman, the leaven of the kingdom. So, far from being lulled into the complacency of the obvious and the expected, this parable is one which can startle and disturb us telling as it does of the breakthrough of God's reign, subverting the text, subverting our world.

I want to turn now to Luke's setting of the same text. I do this to illustrate the importance of context in the interpretation of texts, the need, as I have stressed in other chapters, to remove the brackets which isolate these sayings or stories.

We might notice first that the same pair of parables appears together, that of the mustard seed and that of the leaven. There are slight differences. Luke introduces the pair with questions: 'What is the kingdom of God like?' and 'To what should I compare it?' The parable of the mustard seed follows but with no reference to the comparison between 'the smallest seed' and the 'greatest shrub' as in Matthew. The parable of the leaven also begins with a question, 'And again he said, "To what shall I compare the kingdom of God?"' The rhetorical device of using a question rather than a statement alerts the listener to expect to be surprised.

More important though than the minor textual differences is the setting. Matthew has placed the pair of parables within his day of parables, seven in all, pointing to the kingdom. In Luke's case the parables follow a rather dramatic incident in the synagogue. They are connected to the incident by means of the linking phrase, 'He said therefore . . .' The parables then become a commentary on that event. We could transfer the question, 'What is the kingdom of God like?' to form a preface to the story. It begins with Jesus teaching in one of the synagogues on the Sabbath. A woman enters who is bent over, having been crippled for eighteen years. Jesus calls her over and immediately liberates her, 'Woman, you are set free.' Her prayers become praise. In the controversy which follows, where Jesus is criticised for healing on the Sabbath, he defends his action by arguing for the right of 'this woman, a daughter of Abraham, whom Satan bound for eighteen long years' to be 'set free from this bondage on the Sabbath day'. Shock waves must have passed through the congregation in the synagogue. In one of the most subversive comments in the Gospel, Jesus redefines the religious heritage to include women and redefines the Sabbath as the most appropriate day on which to proclaim and bring liberation.

The writer Walter Wink is eloquent in his interpretation of this text:

> . . . to call her a 'Daughter of Abraham' was to make her a fully fledged member of the covenant and of equal standing before God with men. To heal her on the Sabbath was to liberate the Sabbath to be a jubilee of release and restoration. To touch her

*was to revoke the holiness code with its male scruples about
menstrual uncleanness and sexual advances. To speak to her in
public was to jettison male restraints on women's freedom. . . .
To place her in the middle of the synagogue was to challenge the
male monopoly on the means of grace and access to God.*[7]

So well we might ask, what then is the reign of God like? To
liberate this woman, marginalised by her sex and by her
deformity, is to offer liberation to all who have traditionally been
excluded. The phrase 'Daughter of Abraham' is paralleled in
typically Lucan fashion later when Jesus refers to the despised
tax-collector Zaccheus as 'Son of Abraham'. Salvation comes to
house and temple. The reign of God appears among those
considered least likely to manifest it. It breaks through
restrictions of law, restrictions of class, restrictions of gender.
The call to conversion is made to all who would seek to limit the
offer of God's liberating grace.

And so, what is the reign of God like? It is like a seed which
grows into a tree and the birds come and nest there. But push
out the boundaries just a little further. It is like a woman who
takes yeast, yeast which can corrupt, and mixes it with three
measures of flour until it is all leavened. The woman is preparing
the banquet of the Lord, 'The people will come from east and
west, from north and south, and will eat in the kingdom of
God.' (Luke 13: 29) The understanding of the Sabbath has been
broken open, subverted by the healing of a bent woman who in
her body symbolised the suffering of the Israelites for eighteen
years under the Amonites (Judg. 10: 8). On this hallowed day a
woman is liberated and praises God. She, a daughter of
Abraham who was a symbol of the suffering of her people, is
now a symbol for their liberation. This is a topsy-turvy
kingdom: it disrupts and disturbs. It appears where it is least
expected: through the healing of a crippled woman praying in
the synagogue. Just as the 'holiness' of the Sabbath is apparently
corrupted, defiled by a healing which transforms the whole
concept of 'holy' and of 'sabbath', so the apparently corrupt
leaven transforms the dough.

Little wonder then that Jerusalem will kill the prophet who preaches a reign of God which manifests itself among the least, 'Indeed some who are last will be first, and some are first who will be last.' (Luke 13: 30)

And so, freed from the brackets which marked this parable as a self-explanatory maxim about growth from small beginnings, we have a wonderfully subversive text which turns our understanding of God's reign upside down.

To Luke's warning, 'Beware the yeast of the Pharisees', we might want to add, beware the taming of the text, beware the taming of women! Behold the woman concealing the yeast, behold the woman revealing the reign of God!

CHAPTER 11

INTERRUPTING WOMEN

An account of the birth story of Jesus the Messiah, the son of David, the son of Abraham.

Abraham was the father of Isaac and Isaac the father of Jacob, and Jacob the father of Judah and his brothers, and Judah the father of Perez and Zerah by Tamar, *and Perez the father of Hezron, and Hezron the father of Aram, and Aram the father of Aminadab, and Aminadab the father of Nahshon, and Nahshon the father of Salmon and Salmon the father of Boaz by* Rahab *and Boaz the father of Obed by* Ruth *and Obed the father of Jesse, and Jesse the father of King David.*

And David was the father of Solomon by the wife of Uriah, *and Solomon the father of Rehoboam and Rehoboam the father of Abijah and Abijah the father of Asaph and Asaph the father of Jehoshaphat and Jehoshaphat the father of Joram . . .*

And after the deportation to Babylon: Jechoniah was the father of Salathiel and Salathiel was the father of Zerubbabel, and Zerubabbel was . . .

and Matthan was the father of Joseph the husband of Mary, of whom Jesus was born, who is called the Messiah. (Matt. 1: 1–16)

In the birth story of Jesus forty-one fathers are listed according to the pattern: A was the father of B, B was the father of C and so on. There are no daughters. However to our surprise the pattern is broken by the inclusion of five women, four from the Hebrew Scriptures and then finally Mary who further breaks the pattern when Joseph is named in relation to her, 'husband of Mary', rather than the expected 'wife of Joseph'.

What are they doing there? They interrupt the flow of the narrative, breaking the neat and predictable pattern. They are oddly disruptive and disturbing in a way analogous to the disturbance caused in both text and interpretation by the Canaanite woman.[1]

I want to take a brief look at the stories of each of these women and then ask what their role might be in this birth story. Each story will be told first for its own sake to remember and honour the women who are mentioned and then I will explore their place as interruptions to the narrative.

Tamar has been named in our tradition as a harlot. Her history is more complicated. It is told in Genesis 38. She was chosen as the wife of Er, the son of Judah. After Er died leaving his wife childless Judah ordered his second son Onan to follow the practice of marrying his widowed sister-in-law, Tamar, and 'raising up offspring' for his brother. Onan resisted the idea, and practising one of the most primitive forms of birth control — spilling his semen on the ground — ensured that Tamar would not become pregnant. This displeased the Lord and Onan was put to death. Judah, having seen two of his sons die, was reluctant to give his third son to Tamar and so she is left widowed and childless in her father's house.

Hearing that Judah's wife has died and that Judah will be in a certain place shearing his sheep, Tamar leaves off her widow's garb and disguises herself as a prostitute and waits for Judah. He asks her for sex and promises to send her a kid from his flock, but she insists on a pledge from him. She goes home carrying not alone his seed, but his seal, his cord and his staff. She has taken pledges of 'betrothal' and when the men of Judah return to retrieve these personal goods and exchange them for the promised animal, 'the prostitute' is nowhere to be found. When Tamar's pregnancy is discovered she is condemned as a whore and Judah orders that she should be burned, whereupon she exposes the identity of her 'lover', 'It was the owner of these who made me pregnant.' Judah acknowledges his possessions and her right, 'She is more in the right than I . . .' Onan's refusal to give offspring to Tamar, and Judah's refusal to give her his third son have been countered by Tamar who has taken what was her right.

This is a story about a woman who struggles to survive in a system which is heavily biased against her sex. She may be given as a wife, taken as a whore, and rejected by the men to whom

she is given. She has no control over her destiny. In this story
Tamar subverts the system in her favour so that she can resume
her place in the patriarchal household. She does this by breaking
in to interrupt the story and turn it in her favour. She gives birth
to twin boys and it is through Perez, who pushes past his brother
to be the first-born, that the line to David continues.

Tamar would have faded from the narrative until she herself
takes her place. She, like the Canaanite woman, is not given
bread, but has to reach beneath the table and having done so
establishes her right to a place not only in the household of
Judah but also in the history of the people. Where other mothers
remain invisible she is footnoted — 'by Tamar' — and our
curiosity is aroused and we tell her story again.

Commentators report that for a long time the tradition was
embarrassed by the story of Rahab and many textual variants are
found which attempt to gloss over her profession as a prostitute
and to erase the sexual references. Rahab herself is erased from
the albeit brief introduction to the Book of Joshua in the
Jerusalem Bible, 'all is centred around the heroic figure of
Joshua. . . . Joshua holds the centre of the stage throughout.'[2] It
is in fact Rahab who holds the centre of the stage in Chapter 2
where her actions determine the course of the story. The
Israelites under Joshua are waging a 'holy war' against the
Canaanites and spies are sent to Jericho to view the land. They
sleep in the house of Rahab, the prostitute, whose house
intriguingly is 'on the outer side of the city wall and she resided
within the wall itself' (Josh. 2: 15). The King orders Rahab to
bring out the men who have entered the house. She insists that
the men have already left and hides the Israelites under her roof.
She justifies her actions to them, explaining that her people have
lived in fear 'before you' because of what they have heard. Then
she concludes, 'The Lord your God is indeed God in heaven
above and on earth below.' Like Tamar before her she requests a
pledge in return for her favour which may include but clearly
extends far beyond sexual pleasure. 'Since I have dealt kindly
with you, swear that you will deal kindly with my family.' (In
fact Rahab offers to these men the kind of protection which

traditionally a man would offer to a weak and vulnerable woman. She shelters them under her roof.) She asks for deliverance not just for herself but for her extended family, 'Give me a sign of good faith that you will spare my father and mother, my brothers and sisters, and all who belong to them and deliver our lives from death.' (Josh. 2: 13) Her request is granted. 'Our lives for theirs.' Rahab lets the men down by a rope and instructs them further to hide for three days. The rope by which they gain their freedom will be the rope by which Rahab and her family will be saved — the crimson cord tied in the window will be the sign that this house is to be spared.

Rahab has staked her life on this risky gesture of hospitality to the enemy who now surround the city. 'Now Jericho was shut up inside and out because of the Israelites. No one came out and no one went in.' (Josh. 6: 1–2) Joshua announces that the city will be destroyed and that only Rahab and her people will live. The two men return to the house and bring out all 'her kindred' and 'set them outside the camp of Israel'. The city is burnt and everything in it. 'But Rahab and all who belonged to her Joshua spared. Her family has lived in Israel ever since.' (Josh. 6: 25)

In a story told from the perspective of the winners one loses sight of the victims. The victory of Joshua's army means 'the destruction by the sword of men and women, young and old, oxen, sheep and donkeys'. It is a black and white picture of insiders and outsiders, Israelites and Canaanites. A telling moment in the story comes when a man with a drawn sword approaches Joshua who asks, 'Are you one of us or one of our adversaries?' For Joshua there are only two possibilities — to be 'one of us' or 'one of them', a neat definition of sectarianism! To his surprise the messenger replies, 'Neither; but as a commander of the army of the Lord, I have now come.' For one extraordinary moment the traditional polarities are suspended and transcended. 'What do you command?' asks Joshua. 'Remove the sandals from your feet, for the place where you stand is holy.' (Josh. 5: 13–15)[3] To be 'of the Lord' is to transcend 'them' and 'us' — this is what it means to be holy. Rahab too blurs the sharp distinctions between 'us' and 'them'.

It is significant that she lives within the city walls. She is a person inhabiting the boundaries. Her house is on 'the outer side', 'she resides within the city wall'; and one may presume that her profession as a prostitute keeps her on the social margins also. To protect her family she must bring them inside her house; in order that they may be spared they are brought 'outside' the camp of Israel. Finally we are told that they live 'in' Israel. The movement in and out of the house of Rahab reflects the movement from outsider to insider. Rahab, in offering hospitality to the outsiders — from the perspective of her own people — blurs the line between enemy and guest, and establishes a line between them symbolised by the red cord.

Rahab opens the conversation with Joshua's men in the following way: 'I know the Lord has given you the land, and that dread of you has fallen on us.' The categories of 'you' and 'us' are played out, 'there was no courage left in any of us because of you', but then she, like the messenger, moves into another idiom. 'The Lord your God is indeed God in heaven above and on earth below.' (Josh. 2: 11) Self-interest and self-preservation may motivate Rahab but she moves beyond the bargaining ploys here, she moves out of the 'them' and 'us' and speaks instead of true worship. Like another Canaanite woman in Matthew's Gospel this woman, Rahab, sees beyond the tribal divisions to a Lord who is no longer 'your God' but is 'Lord in heaven above and on earth below'.

So how do we remember Rahab? That she was a 'good' prostitute? As Elizabeth Templeton points out, there is no textual justification for reading her story in that way. 'It may indeed be that in the milieu of the time "Rahab the prostitute" could be uttered as matter of factly as "Rahab the postmistress"!'[4] The point of the story is not her profession, nor indeed her morality in that limited sense, but her place on the margins, her role as insider/outsider which enables her to be a sign of breakthrough. Our modern sensibilities may baulk at the destruction of Jericho but within the conventions of the story it is Rahab who, in the exchange of hospitality rather than hostility, ensures that the red thread which saves her and her people is followed down through the ages and appears again in this genealogy, 'Salmon was the father of Boaz *by Rahab.*'

'Boaz was the father of Obed by Ruth.' There is probably little need to refer other than very briefly to this familiar story. However there are several observations which may be worth making.

The Book of Ruth tells the story of women enclosed in a male world. In literary terms this is literally the case! The book opens by telling of a man, Elimelech, and his wife and two sons. By the end of the first paragraph the woman is left 'without her two sons and her husband'. At the end of the Book of Ruth a son is born, 'And they named him Obed; he became the father of Jesse, the father of David. Now these are the descendants of Perez; Perez became the father of Hezron, Hezron of Ram, Ram of Aminadab, Aminadab of Nahson, Nahson of Salmon, Salmon of Boaz, Boaz of Obed, Obed of Jesse and Jesse of David.' (Ruth 4: 18)

In between these male 'bookends' we have the women's story, the story of Ruth and Naomi. At first the three women travel together but Naomi is anxious to send her daughters-in-law back to their 'mother's house'. Orpah agrees to go but Ruth insists on staying using words of friendship and faithfulness which somewhat ironically — as they are addressed to her mother-in-law — have been taken over and read almost exclusively at marriage ceremonies.

Where you go, I will go
Where you lodge, I will lodge
Your people will be my people
and your God my God. (Ruth 1: 16, 17)

When Boaz the landowner first sees Ruth gleaning in his field he asks, 'To whom does this woman belong?' Women belong not to themselves but to a male kin, but here Ruth is described in relation to Naomi. Boaz offers her protection and gives her instructions for her safety. When her work is done Ruth brings the news of the day back to Naomi who listens and advises her how to proceed. The vulnerability of women without the protection of men is made clear and Naomi devises a plot to ensure security and a future for both of them. Ruth is instructed to go to Boaz by night and in references which have a clear sexual connotation she uncovers his feet and asks him to spread his cloak over her. This time the question of Boaz is no longer, 'To whom does this woman belong?' but 'Who are you?' This time the answer comes equally directly, 'I am Ruth.' For one powerful moment in the story male and female face each other as equals. Very quickly Boaz resumes the role of protector and for the last time Ruth returns to listen to the wisdom of her mother-in-law Naomi. From now on she will be under the protection of Boaz who sits down with 'ten men of the elders of the city' to discuss the case. The women's voices are not entirely drowned out though, and when Ruth conceives and has a son it is the women who come to rejoice with Naomi and to name the child, 'A son has been born to Naomi.' Through Ruth, the line continues.

Ruth, like Rahab and Tamar before her, intervenes to take control of her destiny. Until she encounters Boaz, it is Ruth who takes on the 'male' role of protector, 'Where you go, I will go.' Listening to the wisdom of the older woman Ruth shapes a future for both of them. The conversations between the women are reminiscent of the tongues loosened in the house of Zechariah when he is struck dumb and Elizabeth finds her prophetic voice.[5]

Ruth like Rahab occupies a place on the margins, an outsider by birth and background, a Moabite, brought inside through her marriage. The death of her husband should mark her return to her own people but she insists on staying with Naomi. She continues to be described as 'Ruth the Moabite'. 'Soft' interpretations of the story miss the ambiguities in the relationships and the subversive nature of Ruth's power as she deals with Boaz. She disappears at the end, ironically under the name of the woman whose life she has saved and whose future she has secured. Does she remain for ever a foreigner, an outsider? Does she disappear once she has produced the son and

heir? Or does the story of her loyalty, her *chesed*, her imaging of
the faithfulness of the God of Israel continue to be kept in the
memory of the people of Israel until it echoes again in the
genealogy of Matthew? 'Boaz was the father of Obed *by Ruth.*'

Despite the fact that we know her name, the next woman
mentioned is held between two men, her place in the text
reflecting her story. 'David was the father of Solomon by the
wife of Uriah.' Unlike the other women whose stories we have
told, Bathsheba does not shape her own destiny and is very
much the object rather than the subject of the story. In the story
which determines her fate her name is mentioned only twice:
once to introduce her to David, 'This is Bathsheba, daughter of
Eliam, wife of Uriah the Hittite' (2 Sam. 11: 4); and again when
her child has died we are told, 'David consoled his wife
Bathsheba and went to her and lay with her and she bore a son
and he named him Solomon.' (2 Sam. 12: 24) She speaks only
once, 'The woman conceived and she went and told David,
"I am pregnant."' (2 Sam. 11: 5) The starkness of the
announcement startles us, standing as it does in such sharp
contrast to the traditional annunciations, 'You will bear a son.'
In her one moment of speech Bathsheba calls David to account.
It is clear that she bears no responsibility for the adultery as she
attempts neither to conceal the pregnancy nor to deceive her
husband. It is David who attempts to get Uriah to sleep with his
wife so that the child may appear to be his, and when that fails
he has Uriah killed. Not until Nathan the prophet chastises him
does David begin to recognise that he 'had no pity'.

He is punished and the child conceived, through what we can
presume was the rape of Bathsheba, dies. Now that he has
repented and mourned he can take Bathsheba as his wife and she
can bear him a legitimate son. The next time we hear of
Bathsheba she once again has a role in relation to a man: mother
of Solomon (1 Kgs 1: 11–40; 2: 13–25).

It is not surprising then that her name is not mentioned in
Matthew's genealogy. The point of drawing our attention to the
wife of Uriah, as the mother of Solomon, is not to remember her
but to recall the shame of David, and by contrast the

righteousness of Uriah. The issue of Bathsheba's origins is hardly the point. What is noteworthy is that such a painful episode is not glossed over — simply by naming Solomon as the son of David — but recollected: the mother of Solomon was the wife of Uriah, one who was faithful both to his wife and to his duty and who was betrayed by David. Solomon, remembered as the wise one, is the son of Bathsheba, a woman taken by David for his pleasure and forced into marriage with him. The line drawn back from Jesus to David is a tarnished one.

The breaks in the pattern of the birth story, signalled by the mention of the women, prepare us for the final rupture where Joseph is named not as 'father of Jesus' as we would expect, but as 'the husband of Mary, of whom Jesus was born, who is called the Messiah'.

For the first time a man is described in relation to a woman, 'For the Lord has created a new thing on earth, a woman encompasses a man.' (Jer. 31: 22)[6] It is ironic that Mary thereafter hardly features in the Gospel and that the story of the nativity taken up in Chapter 2 is told from Joseph's perspective. It is Joseph, not Mary, who receives the annunciation from the angel of the Lord; it is Joseph who names the child. In some ways we could read this as the final redeeming of the shame and betrayal of Bathsheba and Uriah by David. Joseph acts with the 'pity' and true righteousness which was lacking in his forefather. The naming of Mary, and of Joseph in relation to her, clearly signals her place in the story of salvation. Unlike the other women mentioned in the genealogy, she is not described as shaping her own destiny, she is given her place, and it is Joseph who must learn to read her story and take his place in relation to her.

It would seem that Matthew's concern is not with gender but with true faithfulness, 'While he was still speaking to the crowds, his mother and his brothers were standing outside, wanting to speak to him. Someone told him, "Look, your mother and your brothers are standing outside, wanting to speak to you." But to the one who had told him this, Jesus replied, "Who is my mother and who are my brothers?" And pointing to his disciples, he said, "Here are my mother and my brothers!

Whoever does the will of my father in heaven is my brother and sister and mother.'" (Matt. 12: 46–50)

Matthew is telling a new birth story, a story where traditional patterns are broken and a new community inclusive of women and men is created, a community based not on the correct line to the forefathers or the foremothers but to the will of God. 'Are you one of them or one of us?' becomes an irrelevant question. Such a community transcends the restrictions of gender and is foreshadowed for us by the interruptions into the genealogy of women such as Tamar, Rahab, Ruth, Bathsheba and Mary, and of the men connected with those women, Uriah and Joseph, whose stories alert us to alternative possibilities.

I do not think that we should attempt to smooth out these interruptions, these somewhat uncomfortable stories, but we should let them stand as odd and disruptive, that they may continue to confound our pieties and our platitudes as we attempt to describe the interruption which was signalled by the prophet Isaiah; 'Look the virgin shall conceive and bear a son, and they shall name him Emmanuel.' (Matt. 1: 23)

CHAPTER 12

SILENCING WOMEN

On the sabbath day we went outside the gate by the river, where we supposed there was a place of prayer; and we sat down and spoke to the women who had gathered there. A certain woman named Lydia, a worshipper of God was listening to us; she was from the city of Thyatira and a dealer in purple cloth. The Lord opened her heart to listen eagerly to what was said by Paul. When she and her household were baptised, she urged us saying, 'If you have judged me to be faithful to the Lord, come and stay at my home.' And she prevailed upon us.

One day, as we were going to the place of prayer, we met a slave girl who had a spirit of divination and brought her owners a great deal of money by fortune-telling. While she followed Paul and us she would cry out, 'These men are slaves of the Most High God, who proclaim to you a way of salvation.' She kept doing this for many days. But Paul very much annoyed, turned and said to the spirit, 'I order you in the name of Jesus Christ to come out of her.' And it came out that very hour.

But when her owners saw that their hopes of making money was gone they seized Paul and Silas and dragged them into the marketplace before the authorities . . . After they had given them a severe flogging they threw them into prison and ordered the jailer to keep them securely . . .

After leaving prison they went to Lydia's home; and when they had seen and encouraged the brothers and sisters there, they departed. (Acts 16: 11–19, 23, 40)

This book opened with a tale of two women, Mary and Elizabeth, connected in destiny and in their shared experience of unexpected pregnancies. The second essay also concerned itself with two women, Martha and Mary, who, even if in disagreement with one another, were connected through their response to Jesus. In this chaper I am going to look at a text about two women who are disconnected in experience and in the narrative. Juxtaposing their stories and telling them against the grain reveals a further complexity in the analysis of gender. The text is taken from the continuation of Luke's story in the Acts of the Apostles.

There is a personal journey for me in revisiting a text which I studied several years ago. I remember at that time writing in glowing terms about the role of Lydia and completely ignoring the slave girl. I was alert only to the presence of a clearly powerful woman of considerable social status and was interested in her place in the text *vis-à-vis* Paul, but the other woman was invisible. I was working to a different agenda, one which did not include a complete analysis of the text from the perspective of gender. Now five years later with considerably sensitised antennae I return appalled at my earlier omission. The text has now become for me a moral tale illustrating — by omission — the insistence from radical Christian feminists that the liberation of some women cannot be achieved at the expense of others.[1]

The named women in Acts are women of social standing, women who out of their means can contribute to the Church. The slave girl does not count — is she not also a woman? I am reminded of the powerful cry of Sojourner Truth, an African-American woman and former slave, who speaking at a convention for the emancipation of women in 1852 challenged the narrow construction of gender by asking, 'Ain't I a woman?'[2]

> *That man over there say*
> *a woman needs to be helped into carriages*
> *and lifted over ditches*
> *and to have the best places everywhere*
> *Nobody ever helped me into carriages*
> *or over mud puddles*
> *or gives me the best places . . .*
> *Ain't I a woman?*

She recognised that the description of women as weak, delicate 'needing to be helped over ditches', might have fitted the privileged white women of that society but was not true of her experience as a black female slave — 'working as hard as any man'. She challenged her audience to reconsider their description of the 'feminine' and recognise in whose interests it was constructed.

When we look at the position of women in the Scriptures we can fall into the same trap of seeing only the named — or at least marked — women in their roles *vis-à-vis* the dominant men, so here Lydia and Paul, for example, and thus we can miss the further layer of race or class which marks a more complex system of oppression. A useful illustration of these dynamics is found by analysing the web of relationships in the story of Abraham, Sarah and Hagar told in Genesis 16 and 21. In the struggle for power Hagar, the slave woman, is cast out by her mistress Sarah and abandoned in the wilderness. In making a critique of the patriarchal structure of the story we come to recognise that it is not simply a matter of the dominance of men over women, but rather entails a whole system of relationships of inequality which creates powerless subordinates. Simply changing the gender of the dominant one does nothing to transform the relationships.

So to return to our text, unless we can connect the fate of Lydia and the slave girl we will run the risk of reinscribing the patterns of dominance which ensure that the powerful control the weak. If we highlight the story of Lydia alone we will privilege the experience of the woman of status over the nameless slave girl. And this is somewhat ironic as a continuation of a story which began in a synagogue in Nazareth where the good news was proclaimed to the poor and the oppressed (Luke 4: 18), and was announced to 'beggars',[3] such as the slave girl.

Our reading then will juxtapose the stories of these two women encountered by Paul. The narrator tells the story in the first person plural to suggest an eye-witness account and although this is a description of a mission by Paul it is interesting that it is framed by references to Lydia. The story begins with the meeting with Lydia (16: 14) and ends with a return visit to her house (16: 40). There are sufficient clues then, even in this androcentric narrative, to suggest that Lydia was a woman of considerable importance. The other fascinating detail is the reference to the place where Lydia is encountered. The all male group of Paul and his companions go to 'a place of prayer' on the Sabbath and speak to the 'women who had gathered there' (16: 12). Was this typical for Jewish women to gather for worship? Is this our earliest example of women-church? One early commentary suggests that Paul must have been rather downhearted when he discovered an exclusively female group! The gentile woman Lydia is described as 'a worshipper of God', thus suggesting that she does not belong to this community but is attracted to them. We are given quite a degree of detail about her — suggesting that her range of influence was considerable. We are told that she was from Thyatira, which is a city in Lydia — and we note that she bears the name of her place of origin — and that she was a seller of dyed purple cloth. She was clearly a woman of means and presumably with a considerable network of contacts. Her location in Philippi placed her in a good trading position and therefore subsequently in a pivotal position for the Church in that place.

She listened to Paul and we are told that the Lord opened her heart and she was baptised together with members of her house. She is the householder and presumably her household consists of other women, men of lower status, children and servants. As a house-church it specifically includes men, 'the brothers' who are encouraged (16: 40), and in an ironic contrast to the place of prayer which was 'women only' fails to mention women here. In a parallel conclusion to Peter's conversion of the gentile Cornelius, Lydia invites Paul to stay in her house. However in this case the word used implies a pressing invitation, the same word used in Chapter 24 of Luke's Gospel when the disciples prevailed upon Jesus to stay with them. In this case her insistence implies a certain reluctance on the part of Paul to commit himself to remaining in the house of gentile Christians. Lydia, again emphasising her status argues, 'If you have judged me to be faithful to the Lord, come and stay at my home.' (16: 15) We are reminded of the encounter between Jesus and the tax-collector, Zaccheus, where the relationship/conversion was confirmed by a house visit, 'I must stay at your house today.' (Luke 19:5) The offer of hospitality — and we can presume table-fellowship — seals discipleship at the house of Zaccheus, at Emmaus, at the house of Cornelius, and now at the house of Lydia. In the case of the latter pair the issue of 'eating with the uncircumcised' is resolved in considerable detail in the house of Cornelius by Peter and confirmed here by Paul's acceptance of the hospitality of Lydia and subsequently when he accepts food from the jailer.

The narrative now turns towards the story of the slave girl. This meeting is also set in the context of the place of prayer where the missionaries had first encountered Lydia.

This time however the woman is not given a name and although she is also described by her 'profession' — fortune-telling — in contrast to Lydia, the dealer in purple goods, this does not make her a woman of means but instead earns considerable money for her owners. Doubly possessed — by a demon and by her masters — used and abused — a metaphor for exploitation — this woman cries out and we wait to see how Paul will respond.

'These men are slaves of the most high God, who proclaim to you a way of salvation' (16: 17) is the cry of the slave girl as she follows Paul. The irony is of course that her words are true and perhaps there is a double irony as she describes the disciples as 'slaves'. She recognises that they too are bound by a force greater than themselves which is driving their mission. This commonality is not recognised by Paul who becomes irritated when her calling out continues for several days and he commands the spirit, 'in the name of Christ Jesus to come out of her' (16: 18). Immediately the spirit leaves the woman and she is silent, or more to the point, she is silenced. The attention of the narrator, and thus the response of the reader, turns away from the slave girl towards 'her owners' who, when they see their hope of making money has gone, seize Paul and Silas and drag them before the authorities. The tables turn as now it is no longer a question of the slave girl disturbing Paul and his companions but of Paul and Silas 'disturbing our city' (16: 20).

The clash of cultures — an issue between Paul and the slave girl — is once again manifested. '[They] are advocating customs that are not lawful for us as Romans to observe.' (16: 21) As Paul and Silas are beaten and thrown into jail we realise that we have been caught up in the momentum of their story and that the slave girl has faded from the text. Her story has disappeared without trace. Used first by her owners for gain she has now been used by the narrator to illustrate the clash between Paul and the Roman authorities, and it is significant that whereas Paul and Silas have a means of redress — 'They have beaten us . . . men who are Roman citizens' (16: 37) — the woman has no claim and no such rights. We can only speculate about her fate. It is not difficult to imagine that the anger turned towards Paul and Silas which resulted in a beating for them was first turned towards the girl. Of what use was a worthless slave particularly as she could no longer make money for her owners? Was she abandoned? Was she killed? The text is silent.

The narrative will return later to the house of Lydia to imply a future for her, even if it is no longer within the text, but the slave girl has been erased, she has served her purpose, she has no future either within this text or beyond it.

It is painful to read her story which surely belongs in the category of 'texts of terror'.[4] We could deal with the abuse of the slave girl by her owners, but what is difficult is to recognise that she is equally maltreated by Paul. There is no indication in the text that this is a healing in any conventional sense. We are clearly told that she is a source of irritation, of annoyance to Paul. She interferes with his preaching. There is no indication of compassion on his part. He does not address her personally or enquire about her needs. He orders the spirit to come out of her, but the girl herself is of no further concern to him. We can compare this episode with the healing of the Gerasene demoniac (Luke 8: 26–39). In that case the expulsion of the demons is described as a positive happening for the man who is later found by the people 'sitting at the feet of Jesus, clothed and in his right mind' (Luke 8: 35). Furthermore he has a future, 'proclaiming throughout the city how much Jesus had done for him' (8: 39).

In contrast, the expulsion of the demon from the slave girl serves the interests of Paul and the interests of the narrator, but not the interests of the girl. In fact it has the opposite effect: it renders her worthless. We long to rewrite the story, to take the slave girl into the house of Lydia, to see her welcomed into this new inclusive Christian community where there is no longer slave nor free. But texts of terror do not have happy endings. This tiny tale carries a large burden: it exposes the misogyny of the teller, perhaps of Paul himself, of the early Church. It exposes a complex web of oppression based on a system of patriarchy where the rights of the owners supersede the rights of other human persons, who may indeed be defined as part of the property. It reveals the flawed disordering of relationships along the lines of gender, race and class. It exposes a limited theology which in serving the interests of one group fails even to notice the oppression of another. It reveals a bias towards the socially advantaged which sits very uncomfortably with the basic thrust of the Gospel. Taking this tale out and reading it against the interest of the narrator in the 'hero', Paul, we find a suffering and silenced servant. When we tell her story we feel unease. We ask why the cosmic forces should come to the aid of Paul with an earthquake 'so violent that the foundations of the prison were shaken' (16: 26), but not even the slightest tremor is felt for the girl. We wonder too why Paul and his followers could not deal with words of truth. We wonder whether the reference to the girl's possession by a demon was not an attempt to demonise her and render her prophecy worthless. We recall the response to the maid, Rhoda, when she brought the news that Peter was miraculously freed from his chains and at the gate, 'You are out of your mind' (12: 15); which reaction in turn reflects the response of the disciples to the news of the resurrection brought by the women, 'it seemed to them an idle tale and they did not believe it' (Luke 24: 11). And what of the four daughters of Philip, the evangelist, who are said to have the gift of prophecy? (21: 9) We never hear them speak although Paul stays there several days, and when a prophecy is spoken to Paul it is by a visiting male prophet, Agabus, who came down from Judea. The slave girl is not alone then in the category of silent or silenced women. Yet at the beginning of Acts Peter defends the apostles from charges of drunken behaviour by citing the prophet Joel:

> *I will pour out my Spirit upon all flesh*
> *and your sons and your daughters shall prophesy*

and he continues,

> *Even upon my slaves, both men and women*
> *in those days I will pour out my Spirit;*
> *and they shall prophesy. (2: 17–18)*

The male apostles are defended, their prophecy is justified, but the prophesy of the slave girl is neither justified nor defended by the apostle nor by the forces of nature. It is true that the Greek text makes it clear that she is possessed by 'a spirit of a python', the prophetic spirit of the Delphic oracle, therefore in Jewish terms idolatrous. But Paul shows no interest in 'opening the heart' of this woman as he had opened the heart of Lydia. There is no attempt to effect a conversion from pagan to Christian prophecy. Because the words which were spoken by the woman were true, this surely could have been an option, as in the case of the Gerasene demoniac who, having been healed, evangelises (Luke 8: 39) or, even more dramatically, as in the case of Paul himself who was transformed from one who ravaged the Church to one who became its most zealous defender. The slave girl is afforded no such opportunity. She may be freed from her demon, to satisfy the needs of Paul; she is certainly not freed for any purpose.

In order to critique the text we must read Luke against Luke.[5] What has happened to the prophetic words of Mary, 'he has brought down the powerful from their thrones and lifted up the lowly' (Luke 1: 52) or, as already mentioned, what has happened to the prophetic words of Isaiah taken up by Jesus in the synagogue, 'he has anointed me to bring the good news to the poor . . . to let the oppressed go free' (Luke 4: 18)? To whom is the good news proclaimed in Luke-Acts? Following the conversion of Lydia we are told of the success of the mission in Thessalonica, 'Some of them were persuaded and joined Paul and Silas, as did a great many of the devout Greeks and not a few of the leading women.' (17: 4) Likewise in Beroea, 'Many of them therefore believed, including not a few Greek women and men of high standing.' (17: 12) 'Not a few' suggests many, so we can take it that the converts include many wealthy women and men. The thrust of the Gospel has shifted from the concern for the poor to the need to convert the gentiles. Bringing the Gospel to the gentiles is the major preoccupation of the writer of Acts and it appears to take place through the conversion of certain influential figures who bring their households with them, Lydia and Cornelius being the prime examples. In doing this it is not only the widows who 'are being neglected' (6: 1) but poor females of no status.

If we move away from the stories of Lydia and the slave girl to take a brief look at the role of women in Acts in general, we can begin to see a pattern. It seems clear that women are welcome as long as they perform the prescribed supporting role to the central ministry of the male apostles. This role was signalled early on in Luke's Gospel, when we were told of the women who accompanied Jesus and the twelve, providing 'for them out of their resources' (Luke 8: 3). In Acts we observe a continuation of this restricted role for women and a further barrier of class distinction. Women are counted among those gathered in the upper room 'devoting themselves to prayer' (1: 14) and among those converted by Peter (5: 14), persecuted by Paul (8: 3), and as in the case of Ananias and Sapphira, punished for deceiving the community (5: 1–11). They are thus equally regarded as followers, subjects of male leadership. Tabitha, known for her 'good works and acts of charity' probably represents Luke's ideal female disciple (9: 36–43). Indeed she is the only woman to be named as a disciple. She is the passive recipient of Peter's healing; she does not speak. The only female leader to receive a mention in Acts is Priscilla who, together with her husband Aquila, accompanies Paul to Ephesus. Priscilla is clearly a teacher and preacher of the Gospel correcting the 'eloquent and well-versed' Jew, Apollos, 'but when Priscilla and Aquila heard him, they took him aside and explained the Way of God to him more accurately' (18: 26). We are left open-mouthed and want to hear more of this theological instruction by a woman, but the pair have fulfilled their purpose and the story moves on without them. So it is not Luke in Acts, but Paul in his letters, who pays due tribute to the work of this pair of 'equal disciples', 'Greet Prisca and Aquila who work with me in Christ Jesus' (Rom. 16: 3) and 'Aquila and Prisca, together with the church in their house, greet you . . .' (1 Cor. 16: 19)

Luke's preoccupation is with the mission to the gentiles and his agenda does not include the ministry of women; so the tantalising glimpses that we are given into the role of women cannot create a full picture of the importance of their role in the early Church.[6] However it does seem clear that the primary function served by women was to support the ministry of men. Women like Lydia who did so are rewarded by the presence of the disciples in their houses. Women who prophesy, who are considered to be disruptive — like the slave girl — are silenced and erased from the story of salvation. (No counter-conversion here as with the Canaanite or the Syro-Phoenician woman!) So we cannot speak in general about 'women in Acts' without taking into account the utterly divergent experiences of both Lydia and the slave girl. The inclusion of the story of the slave girl in the story of Lydia did not, alas, result in an inclusion in her household. We cannot find in one story the threads of another as we did previously in the interpolated stories of the woman with the haemorrhage and the daughter of Jairus. Here the story of the slave girl casts a dark and painful shadow across the conversion of Lydia. It serves to challenge us to resist any simplistic description of 'Women and the Church' whether in looking back, or in turning our focus towards the present situation. It reminds us to be alert to the complex intersection of culture and class as well as gender in any such analysis. It keeps before us the provocative cry of Sojourner Truth, 'Ain't I a woman?'

CHAPTER 13

DISBELIEVING WOMEN

But on the first day of the week, at early dawn, they came to the tomb, taking the spices that they had prepared. They found the stone rolled away from the tomb, but when they went in, they did not find the body. While they were perplexed about this suddenly two men in dazzling clothes stood beside them. The women were terrified and bowed their faces to the ground, but the men said to them, 'Why do you look for the living among the dead? He is not here, but has risen. Remember how he told you while he was still in Galilee, that the Son of Man must be handed over to sinners, and be crucified, and on the third day rise again.' Then they remembered his words, and returning from the tomb, they told all this to the eleven and to all the rest. Now it was Mary Magdalene, Joanna, Mary the mother of James, and the other women with them who told this to the apostles. But these words seemed to them an idle tale, and they did not believe them. (Luke 24: 1–11)

A friend of mine argues that this moment of male disbelief of the witness of the women is where the rot set in in the early Church, a rot which has never been eradicated. 'But these words seemed to them an idle tale, and they did not believe them.' Luke follows this account with the story of Peter entering the tomb and leaving amazed, an action which prepares the reader for the comment later on: 'The Lord has risen indeed and he has appeared to Simon!' (Luke 24: 34)

In Mark's Gospel women encircle the final acts of the story — from the unnamed woman who anoints the head of Jesus, the servant girl who draws the confession from Peter, the women who watch the death of Jesus and finally to the women who come to the tomb. Yet this Gospel finishes on a strange and abrupt note as the women flee the empty tomb, 'for terror and amazement had seized them; and they said nothing to anyone for they were afraid' (Mark 16: 8).

Both of these endings are in contrast to the resurrection appearances of Jesus to the group of women, including Mary Magdalene, described in Matthew's Gospel, and to Mary Magdalene alone as told by John, 'Do not be afraid, go and tell my brothers to go to Galilee; there they will see me.'(Matt. 28: 10) 'Go to my brothers and say to them, "I am ascending to my Father and your Father, to my God and your God."' (John 20: 17)

So it looks at first as if we have two different traditions in the early Church: Luke followed by Paul (1 Cor. 15: 5) describes Peter as the first witness to the resurrection; Matthew and John take Mary Magdalene as the first to 'see the risen Lord'. Mark leaves us with an ambiguous ending and Luke clearly suppresses the witness of the women.

Feminist scholars have written damning indictments of Luke's erasure of women, particularly in view of the influence of this apparently benign Gospel on Church teaching and practice.[1] Women through the ages have been praised for their submissive and silent stance, women have been seen and not heard, women have deferred to the importance of men, women religious have lived by the rule of men, women have had their witness checked by men. Yet I wonder is that the only possible reading? Can this text be subverted to yield a blessing?

But first I want to return briefly to Mark and his so abrupt and apparently unsatisfactory ending. Even from the earliest stages of transmission, editors were unhappy about the ending and, unable to return it to the author with a request that it be rewritten, they did the job themselves, and so our Bibles contain several alternative endings. But what happens if we hold to the starkness of 16: 8? 'They said nothing to anyone for they were afraid.' The reader, or listener, instead of being gently lulled into the conclusion of the story, is jolted awake by the abruptness and surprise of a conclusion which fails to conclude. The story of Mark resists being held in the past and breaks through to a time beyond the text.[2] The breakthrough of resurrection does not mark an end but a new beginning. The fear expressed by the women is legitimate and justified and in the light of Mark's

Gospel is probably the prelude to greater faith, 'I believe, help my unbelief.' (Mark 9: 24)

The purpose of this brief return to Mark's ending is to suggest that it is a mistake to rush to premature conclusions, particularly about premature endings! The secrets of Mark's Gospel are broken open in the most surprising ways. The women disciples do not desert, deceive, betray or even misunderstand as the male disciples do. They are the ones who faithfully remain at the cross and who come to the tomb. It is they who find themselves on the threshold of the inbreaking of divine power, 'He has been raised. He is not here.' It is little wonder that they flee terrified. And it is not without irony that we note that 'they said nothing to anyone' is contradicted by the telling of the story to which they alone are the witnesses!

So back to Luke. Here too I suggest that irony is the key. It is certainly the key that unlocks the story which follows, that of the disciples on the road to Emmaus. Once again we must remove the brackets which could suggest that the story of the women ends with the disbelief of the apostles. In fact this is clearly not the case as the Emmaus narrative refers back to the women's story. 'Moreover some women of our group astounded us . . .' (Luke 24: 22) The conversation on the road to Emmaus gives us the context within which the witness of the women can be interpreted. In fact that journey to Emmaus provides us with the interpretive grid according to which the whole Gospel is read.

It is perhaps the most brilliant example of the art of Luke's storytelling and works rather like a set of Russian dolls where each layer conceals and then reveals another, except of course in this case the final revelation is not the smallest but the greatest moment, experienced as a flash of illumination which transforms all that has gone before.

It has been described as 'a parable about interpretation'.[3] We, as readers, are drawn into the experience through the disciples as they attempt to assimilate the events of the last days with their own experience and expectations of Jesus. It illustrates the process of hermeneutics at work. The disciples, the interpreters, have their frame of reference, their presuppositions, and their story which, as it is told, is exposed to alternative perspectives until the same events are shaped differently as they are reinterpreted.

The story opens with 'two of them' going to Emmaus about seven miles from Jerusalem. The text does not tell us whether these two disciples were both male, or male and female. One argument in favour of the latter interpretation is that where the man is named, here Cleopas, the unnamed one is likely to be female. Some scholars suggest that it may be Mary the wife of Cleopas mentioned in John's Gospel (19: 25). Against that possibility it could be argued that Luke regularly refers to male and female pairs, usually naming both. However we can leave open the possibility that 'some women of our group' might include this woman whose witness had been dismissed. In any case these two are deeply concerned about what has happened and are discussing these events when they are joined by Jesus. They are so preoccupied with the past, with what 'had happened' that they do not notice what is happening. The narrator tells us that 'their eyes were kept [held] from recognising him' (24: 16). The irony of the story works only because it plays on the superior knowledge of the reader who is drawn into the plot by the narrator. Like the child watching Punch and Judy we want to shout out, 'Look behind you!' or rather 'Look in front of you!' But this kind of blindness is not susceptible to logic but requires a different form of healing. The stranger asks about the topic of conversation and we are told, 'They stood still, looking sad.' One imagines that their eyes are fixed on the ground. Their sorrow has immobilised them. With beautiful irony, Cleopas asks, 'Are you the only stranger in Jerusalem who does not know the things which have taken place in these days?' The 'stranger' then draws out their story about the prophet, mighty in word and deed, and how he was handed over to be condemned to death and crucified and how they 'had hoped that he was the one to redeem Israel'. The tense is revealing: their hope is locked in the past. That story also holds the story of the women, told from the perspective of the male disciples, 'Some women of our group astounded us . . . Some of those who were with us went to the tomb, and found it just as the women had said; but they did not see him.' (24: 22–4) It is at this point that the stranger interrupts them, 'Oh, how foolish you are and slow of heart to believe all that the prophets have declared!' So at the very point when the disciples tell of their inability to trust the women, they are sharply reprimanded. Thus the story told at the tomb to the women and more importantly remembered by them and reported by them to the eleven — and disbelieved — is repeated and confirmed here. 'Was it not necessary that the Messiah should suffer these things and then enter into his glory?' (24: 26) 'The idle tale' is taken up and expounded by the 'stranger' who, beginning with the prophets, interprets 'the things about himself in all the scriptures'. The hermeneutical process continues as the limited perspective according to which these disciples had read the events is broadened to include a different interpretation. The story told by the women is taken up and interpreted within the framework of the 'stranger's story' which becomes the story of salvation.

So now we have a cluster of stories — the appearance to the women, the experience of Peter, the expectations of the disciples — woven together to shape a different story which will be affirmed by the events which follow. Continuing the 'play' of the narrative we are told that when they reach the village Jesus walks ahead 'as if he were going on' (24: 28). In pressing 'the stranger' to accept their hospitality the disciples demonstrate that they have heard and received 'the word'. They are now ready to receive this stranger as 'guest'.

In the brilliant climax of the story the moment of recognition, the moment of presence — at the breaking of the bread — is paradoxically a moment of absence: 'Their eyes were opened, and they recognised him; and he vanished from their sight.' Once their eyes are opened to see and understand — to insight — they no longer need to see outwardly. The darkness of the empty tomb is suffused with the light of the resurrection. The 'idle tale' has been revealed as truly astounding.

The words used to describe the actions at the table, the taking, blessing, breaking and giving of the bread recall the feeding at Bethsaida. There too the day was drawing to a close, but in that situation the disciples suggested that the crowd should be sent away. Here they have remembered the instruction, 'You give them something to eat.' (9: 13) In offering hospitality, it is offered to them as the one they invite as guest becomes the host. The breaking of bread is the final key which unlocks the events of the story and which gathers them and illuminates them. 'Were not our hearts burning within us while he was talking to us on the road and opening the scriptures to us.' (24: 32)

All is now connected. The separate strands of the story, or better, the separate stories come together to shape a new story in a place which had looked like the journey's end but, continuing the paradoxical surprise of the story, becomes the beginning! So those original moments of closure need to be revisited and reinterpreted in the light of the events at Wisdom's table at Emmaus: the crucifixion when 'darkness came over the whole land' (23: 44), the empty tomb where 'they did not find the body' (24: 2), the disbelief of the eleven, 'but these words seemed to them an idle tale' (24: 11), and the despair of the disciples, 'We had hoped . . .' In recognising the presence of Jesus at the table, in the breaking of the bread, all these events and experiences are reinterpreted in the light of faith. The blindness of the outer eye is countered by the inner eye of faith.

There is now a new story to be shared with the others and the once disconsolate disciples now return energised to Jerusalem.

There is a moment of anticlimax as before they can tell their tale their companions get in first, 'The Lord has risen indeed, and has appeared to Simon.'(24: 34) The need to establish the priority of Peter would seem to allow for the possibility that the Emmaus disciples included a woman. It could be read as evidence for the ongoing struggle between the two different traditions, with Luke anxious to lay down his marker for the prior appearance to Peter, or at least to use the appearance to Peter to confirm the story of the women which is not accepted on its own merits. However, if that is the case, he succeeds only on one level, the literal factual level. The appearance to Peter, stated but not narrated, has no power of conviction, whereas the story of the disciples on the road to Emmaus utterly captivates us. Its power convinces us, converts us. Like the disciples on the road, we too are turned around by it! So if once again we read Luke against Luke, it is not Peter who bears the good news of the resurrection but two disciples, one named Cleopas, the other unnamed and possibly a woman! And even if that fragile possibility is too tenuous to support the place of women, there is no doubt that the witness and the story of the women remembered and reported by them is the same story which is vindicated by the stranger and ultimately causes the hearts of the disciples 'to burn within them'. The stone which is rejected becomes the cornerstone; the idle tale which is dismissed is the good news.

The male disciples were reprimanded because they had failed to believe 'all that the prophets had declared' (24: 25). We are reminded of the beginning of the Gospel when Zechariah's failure to believe was punished and he was struck dumb, and into his silence came the prophetic exchanges of Elizabeth and Mary. Now at the end of the Gospel we witness the blindness of the disciples who see, '[they] found it just as the women had said; but they did not see him' (24: 24), but fail to understand. Once again the women are prepared to accept the divine messengers but they fail to convince the others. Although the truth of their story is demonstrated, the power of their witness and their faith is not explicitly acknowledged or praised. Between the lines of the reprimand, 'O foolish disciples', we have to read the invisible script, 'O wise women, who have not seen but have believed.'

As I have struggled with a story which I freely admit I delight in for so many reasons, I am aware that I cannot let it go without insisting on a blessing! The narrator of Luke's Gospel may have been blind to the considerations of gender or there may indeed have been an effort in the Lucan community to suppress the ministry of women, but despite that, the power of the Emmaus story explodes beyond gender. If we read it as a parable about interpretation then it invites all of us, male or female, Jew or gentile, slave or free, to acknowledge the limitations of our particular context, our particular perspective. Listening to the stories of others invites us to the conversion of seeing differently and of recognising the story of the other not as threat, 'an idle tale', but as a gift leading ultimately to the experience of a communion which embraces our plurality of stories in a unity which holds and transcends our differences.

Emmaus is not the journey's end and read in this way it does not represent the final closure on the story of women, but instead invites us to a new beginning. The process of telling and retelling which forms the community narrative, 'Then they told what had happened . . .' is an ongoing one. And in our time the stories of women are radically reshaping that narrative.

Epilogue

Tell all the truth but tell it slant —
Success in Circuit lies
Too bright for our infirm Delight
the Truth's superb surprise

As Lightning to the children eased
With explanation kind
The Truth must dazzle gradually
Or every man be blind —

Emily Dickinson (1830–86)[1]

Emily Dickinson's quite brilliant poem is printed without comment at the front of this book. It is there as a kind of marker and, for me, as a reminder of how I wanted to write. I very much wanted to 'tell the truth', but have come to recognise that 'telling it slant' is particularly apt for a perspective on scripture which seeks to be faithful both to the text and to women. I like the idea too of the 'truth' dazzling gradually, as insight is not something which comes instantly but is rather the result of close attention — both to the text and to one's own experience. In many of the scripture stories of the healing of the blind there is a progression from blindness to sight and finally to insight.

I am nervous about endings, suspicious of that final authoritative statement which closes down the discussion. Perhaps I have too often been on the receiving end of such closures! So in a sense I would like my conclusion to resemble the shorter and earliest ending of Mark's Gospel, 'And they said nothing to anyone for they were afraid.' (Mark 16: 8) This is not as negative as might first appear — first because its abruptness leaves the ending open and secondly because the very existence of the Gospel of Mark contradicts the idea that 'they said nothing'! But perhaps even more revealing was a comment from a woman at a workshop in Antrim in the North of Ireland. We had been reading this Gospel and discussing the role of the women and, having puzzled over the ending, this woman finally announced, 'I've got it! They may have said nothing when they left the empty tomb, but you can be sure they told everyone when they got home!' It was a wonderful and refreshing insight and rang true to the experience of these women.

So this is not a conclusion but an epilogue. It hopes to leave the door open so that the conversations may continue, but at the same time I want to gather some reflections together and revisit the more fundamental question of why stay with these Scriptures at all. Looking back over these essays I am aware of the extent to which I have absorbed Phyllis Trible's notion of struggling with the text like Jacob with the angel, refusing to let go without a blessing. I have insisted even in the most unlikely of texts — Luke's account of the resurrection (Chapter 13), or Matthew's tale of the Canaanite woman (Chapter 4) — on a blessing.

The darkest shadow was cast by the story of Lydia and the slave girl (Chapter 12) and it was probably the clearest example of the need to read scripture against itself. I have no doubt that some critics will consider my approach too benign, a form of patching. For some the whole Bible is a 'text of terror', keeping women in a state of perpetual subjugation. They see no option but to abandon it.

For me there is too much at stake. Sacred Scripture, like the tradition of the Church itself, is my birthright and has been a source both of pain and of liberation. There is a poem by the American poet, Adrienne Rich, entitled 'Power' which captures the ambivalence which I feel. It begins:

> Today I was reading about Marie Curie:
> She must have known she suffered from radiation sickness
> her body bombarded for years by the element
> she had purified . . .

Rich tries to understand how this woman could have ignored the signs of her illness, her cataracts, her cracked skin and so on. She concludes:

She died a famous woman denying
her wounds
denying
her wounds came from the same source as her power.[2]

That 'her wounds came from the same source as her power' seems to me a brilliant and useful metaphor for women reading scripture. The image from Phyillis Trible carries something of the same idea because when Jacob finally emerges into the dawn after his night-long struggle with the angel he too is wounded and limping. So we are talking about costly grace and hard-won blessing. This is about accepting limitation, recognising that these texts arose in a particular context, which inevitably rendered them patriarchal. The difficulty arises of course from their status as revelatory.

Yet there too I think we can be helped by the realisation that revelation is not always benign. The texts can reveal pain, terror, difficulty, or even sheer ambiguity, but what they consistently reveal is the attempt of a people to read the scripts of their lives as witnessing to the presence of God and that often flawed attempt continues today. Women questioning the place to which they have been relegated are now demonstrating a new confidence about clearing space for themselves — a place where they can recognise and lay claim to their own experience of God's presence in their lives.

One of the practical ways in which the kind of work undertaken in this book might help is in affirming that new 'sense of place'. Women who proclaim the Scriptures in a liturgical setting will now do so 'knowingly'. My experience in workshops with women on scripture and gender has demonstrated the power of even hearing the word in a different voice. Some women listening on one occasion were amazed at how they heard the familiar words as a different story when proclaimed with a consciousness of the issues. To read from the perspective of the woman within the text and from the experience of the woman outside the text is already a new interpretation.

There is another reason, already briefly mentioned in the Preface, why I am reluctant to abandon this work. Leaving aside for a moment the status of these texts as 'Sacred Scripture' they are quite simply classic texts. One of my great pleasures when I started to study theology as a mature student several years ago was the discovery of scripture as literature. Texts which until then had remained within the pages of a dusty book, or had been experienced as oddly truncated readings in church, suddenly came alive as literary texts. Some vague notion of Bible study as a rather dull, devotional exercise gave way to an exciting exploration of fascinating stories and theories of interpretation. Without any knowledge or indeed interest at that time in the perspective of gender, I began to read the Scriptures. The teasing paradox of the parables, the stark simplicity of Mark's narrative, the rich symbolism of the Gospel of John, the consistent metaphor of the meal in the Gospel of Luke all delighted and fascinated me. So when I discovered the feminist perspective it was in the first place another way of reading. It opened up dimensions which I had not previously seen. It has now become impossible for me to read without this perspective and of course it spills over from the text into the contemporary context.

So there remains for me this double commitment to which I have already referred, the attempt to be faithful on two fronts: to the texts of scripture and to the scripts being written today of the lives of women.

In a book with the teasing title *Swallowing a Fishbone?* Daphne Hampson and other feminist theologians debate Christianity.[3] Hampson, who edits the book, has extricated herself from Christianity. For her it is the fishbone that sticks in her throat and threatens to choke her. She refuses to swallow it. What is interesting is that the other five contributors come from diverse positions within Christianity. I am drawn to their work because it represents the community of women who, like the Canaanite woman, make a nuisance of themselves and cause a disturbance. The dimension which is very often missing in these discussions, and which I have found so often in my teaching, is humour. It is a great leveller. It puts everything, even gender, into perspective and regularly, as illustrated in my opening anecdote, releases not only tension but also insight.

I was present with a friend recently at a celebration of the Eucharist in a church where there is no attempt to use inclusive language. The issue does not arise. The final hymn referred to 'Jacob's sons and daughters'. I was so surprised at the inclusion of 'daughters' that it registered immediately, as did the reason which was clear from the following lines — 'Daughters' were needed to rhyme with 'Red Sea waters'! 'Typical,' commented my friend afterwards. 'Women are included when they are needed to rhyme or chime with men!

However the real delight comes in teasing out the possibilities in the texts rather than scoring points about the rather obvious gender deficiencies. The apparently domestic allusion to the woman mixing yeast into the flour (Chapter 10) is a case in point. The parable told against the grain became a surprising, subversive revelation of God's reign. Scripture scholar Nicola Slee, one of the contributors to Daphne Hampson's book, suggests reading the whole story of Jesus as a parable in order '. . . not merely to legitimise, but to demand a kind of tensile, broken and reforged relation to authoritative religious texts and traditions, which is the only possible kind of relation women can maintain with mainstream religion in our time . . . to read the story of Jesus as a parable challenges women readers to a radical narrative reconstruction of our understandings of self, world and God respectively.'[4] Slee draws on the understanding of the parable as a means of subverting structures, of disorienting and reorienting the reader. Thus they provide an appropriate metaphor for women reading the Scriptures. She offers one answer to the question about the consequences for women today. There is no blueprint to be followed from the Gospels in relation to contemporary questions about sexism for example, but the method of engagement with the texts can in itself free women readers from seeking explanation or closure and can invite them to complete the script in their own lives. The challenge works both ways: women questioning the Scriptures find the Scriptures questioning them.

I very much like the suggestion of a broken and reforged relationship to the text and to the tradition. It is somewhat analogous to my attempt to subvert the text and to remove stories about women from the safe domestic confines to which they have often been relegated and expose them to a wider context. The personal and private becomes political and public. The experience can be unsettling as the following anecdote illustrates. Having explored the story of Mary and Martha along the lines indicated in Chapter 2, one woman looked rather unhappy at the end of the session. 'Are you all right?' I asked. 'Well,' she responded, 'I was much happier with that story before you got at it!' It is unsettling when the accustomed grooves, well-worn even by complaint, are disturbed, and readings are destabilised and we wonder whether we will be left clinging to the wreckage on open seas without a guide. My response to that is that the narratives of the New Testament are meant to be disturbing and destabilising. One could argue that one of the gifts of the feminist perspective is to recover that original intent. Again as Nicola Slee points out the identity of Jesus is 'broken and remade on the cross and similarly fractured and "re-membered" in every contemporary retelling'.[5] These essays have taken up familiar stories and fractured and re-membered them differently. The activity does not rest with exposing the fault-lines of gender gaps but is also concerned with revealing the grace-lines — beyond gender.

So there may be no return to an innocent or naive reading of scripture, but equally there is no return to the stifled yawns of boredom, 'There was once a man . . .' Words which for years have sat solidly on pages now leap out and confront us! Sentences and paragraphs which formed themselves in an orderly fashion now reveal gaps and silences and we read between every line. There is a certain playfulness as we engage with stories from which stones have been lifted and that opening of the imagination frees women from their initial fear and trembling and the stories pour out painfully, passionately, joyfully. The dark night, the empty tomb have not been avoided but have been confronted. And in the truest paradox of the

Christian Gospel it is precisely in facing fear and darkness that light and life can come.[6] The displaced women return home and truly know their place for the first time.

Notes

Introduction: Reading from a Feminist Perspective

1. This piece, 'Christ in the House of Martha and Mary', is due to be published in Autumn 1998 in *Elementals*, a collection of short stories by A.S. Byatt.
2. David Tracy, *Plurality and Ambiguity: Hermeneutics, Religion, Hope*, SCM Press 1987, 12.
3. See Chapter 13 for a development of this idea.
4. Tracy, op. cit., 15.
5. One example of such a re-reading is found in the short story, 'Conversation Piece', by George Steiner, *Proofs and Three Parables*, Faber & Faber 1992.
6. Trible uses the image of Jacob wrestling with the angel as a metaphor for her feminist reading of scripture in *Texts of Terror: Literary Feminist Readings of Biblical Narratives*, SCM Press 1992, 1984, 4.
7. Sandra Schneiders, *Beyond patching: Faith and Feminism in the Catholic Church*, Paulist Press 1991, 56.
8. Cited in 'Transforming the Legacy' by Elisabeth Schussler Fiorenza, and see also the essay by Karen Baker Fletcher in *Searching the Scriptures: Volume One, A Feminist Introduction*, edited by Elisabeth Schussler Fiorenza, SCM 1994.
9. See *Hear Our Voice: Women Rabbis Tell Their Stories*, edited by Sibyl Sheridan, SCM 1994 and *Silence in Heaven: A Book of Women's Preaching* edited by Heather Walton and Susan Durber, SCM 1994.

Chapter 1: Visiting Women

1. See, for example, the story of Sarah and Hagar (Gen. 16; 21) and Penninah and Hannah (1 Sam. 1). Barbara Reid makes the same point in *Choosing the Better Part?: Women in the Gospel of Luke*, The Liturgical Press 1996, 73.
2. Brigitte Kahl, 'Towards a Materialist-Feminist Reading' in *Searching the Scriptures: Volume One, A Feminist Introduction*, edited by Elisabeth Schussler Fiorenza, SCM 1993, 237.
3. Sara Maitland, 'Ways of Relating' in *Feminist Theology: A Reader*, edited by Ann Loades, SPCK 1990, 148, 149.

Chapter 2: Serving Women

1. Although I too have chosen passages about women, I will try to read them in context and to integrate the stories within the larger whole.
2. As argued by Jane Schalberg in her commentary on Luke in *The Women's Bible Commentary*, edited by Carol A. Newson and Sharon Ringe, SPCK 1992, and Elisabeth Schussler Fiorenza in *But She Said: Feminist Practices of Biblical Interpretation*, Beacon Press Boston 1992, 52–76.
3. A phrase used by Phyllis Trible to describe the reading of difficult texts.

Chapter 3: Suffering Women

1.   See reference in Elizabeth Johnson, *She Who Is: The Mystery of God in Feminist Theological Discourse*, Crossroad 1992, 264.

Chapter 4: Disturbing Women

1.   Sharon H. Ringe, 'A Gentile Woman's Story' in *Feminist Interpretation of the Bible*, edited by Letty Russell, Westminster Press 1985, 69.
2.   See Daniel Harrington in *Sacra Pagina: The Gospel of Matthew*, Sacra Pagina Series, Vol. 1, a Michael Glazier Book, Liturgical Press 1991, 237.
3.   Ringe, op. cit., 65.
4.   Sandra Schneiders, *Beyond patching: Faith and Feminism in the Catholic Church*, Paulist Press 1991, 108.

Chapter 5: Feeding Women

1.   Daniel J. Harrington, *The Gospel of Matthew*, Sacra Pagina Series, Vol. 1 (a Michael Glazier Book, published by the Liturgical Press 1991) 220.
2.   Francis Moloney, *A Body Broken for a Broken People: Eucharist in the New Testament*, Collins Dove 1990, 42.
3.   Moloney, op. cit., 42.
4.   For a development of this idea, see Elaine Wainwright, 'The Gospel of Matthew', in *Searching the Scriptures* Vol. 2: *A Feminist Commentary*, edited by Elisabeth Schussler Fiorenza, SCM Press 1994.

Chapter 6: Remembering Women

1.   In particular with the publication of Elisabeth Schussler Fiorenza, *In Memory of Her: A Feminist Theological Reconstruction of Christian Origins*, SCM Press 1983.
2.   For a discussion of the position of women at meal settings in the Gospels, see the comprehensive work of Kathleen Corley, *Private Women, Public Meals: Social Conflict in the Synoptic Tradition*, Hendrikson Massachusetts 1993.
3.   See Chapter 3 for a fuller discussion.

Chapter 7: Confronting Women

1.   *The Woman's Bible Commentary*, 266.
2.   See Chapter 4 for an extensive treatment of this incident as told in Matthew's Gospel.

Chapter 8: Placing Women

1.   See Chapter 6.
2.   Barbara Reid, *Choosing the Better Part* (118–23) argues that the term 'prostitute' was used as a slur against women who overstepped societal roles. However her argument does not seem convincing in this case with the very

obvious eroticism. In contrast, see Kathleen Corley, *Private Women Public Meals*, 'Only slaves or prostitutes would perform such a function in the context of a meal.' 125.

3. Barbara Reid, *Choosing the Better Part*, 122.
4. A phrase used by John R. Donahue, S.J., *The Gospel in Parable*, Fortress Press: Philadelphia, 134.
5. Sean Freyne, *Galilee, Jesus and the Gospels*, Gill & Macmillan: Dublin 1988, 100.

Chapter 9: Missing Women

1. Marcus Borg, *The God we never knew: Beyond dogmatic religion to a more authentic faith*, HarperCollins 1997, 116.
2. For a good analysis of this problem, see Elizabeth Johnson, *She Who Is*, 50–54.
3. Marcus Borg, *Meeting Jesus Again for the First Time*, Harper San Francisco 1994, 48.
4. Sandra Schneiders, *Women and the Word*, Paulist Press 1986, 46.
5. John R. Donahue, *The Gospel in Parable*, Fortress Press 1988, 151.
6. A Phrase used by Marcus Borg in *Meeting Jesus*, 58.
7. Barbara Reid makes this point in *Choosing the Better Part*, 183. The same point is made by John R. Donahue, op. cit., 149.
8. Sandra Schneiders, op. cit., 59.
9. Elizabeth Johnson, *She Who Is*, 160.

Chapter 10: Concealing Women

1. Susan Praeder, *The Word in Women's Worlds: Four Parables*, Zaccheus Studies: New Testament, Michael Glazier 1988, 18.
2. As suggested, for example, by Barbara Reid in *Choosing The Better Part*, 171.
3. Elizabeth David, *English Bread and Yeast Cookery*, Penguin Books 1979, 90.
4. For example, see Praeder, op. cit., 28.
5. Luke Timothy Johnson, *The Gospel of Luke*, Sacra Pagina Series, Vol. 3, Michael Glazier, The Liturgical Press, Collegeville, Minnesota 1991, 213.
6. Praeder, op. cit., 32.
7. Walter Wink, *Engaging the Powers: Discernment and Resistance in a World of Domination*, Fortress Press 1992, 129.

Chapter 11: Interrupting Women

1. This story is discussed in Chapter 4.
2. *The New Jerusalem Bible*, Darton Longman and Todd 1985, 276.
3. See Danna Nolan Fewell's commentary on the Book of Joshua in *The Women's Bible Commentary*, 63.
4. Elizabeth Templeton, 'Rahab The Prostitute' in *Silence in Heaven*, 105.
5. See Chapter 1
6. For a discussion of this phrase, see Phyllis Trible, 'God and the Rhetoric of Sexuality', SCM Press 1992, 47–56.

Chapter 12: Silencing Women

1. See, for example, Elisabeth Schussler Fiorenza, 'Justa — Constructing Common Ground', in *But SHE Said: Feminist Practices of Biblical Interpretation*, Beacon Press 1992, 114–20.
2. Cited in various sources including Margaret Busby, *Daughters of Africa*, Jonathan Cape 1992; Vintage 1998.
3. On this point, see Philip Francis Esler, *Community and Gospel in Luke-Acts: The Social and Political Motivations of Lucan Theology*, Cambridge University Press, 164, who argues that the correct translation of the Greek (ptōchos) is 'beggars' and that the force of that is eviscerated by the translation 'the poor'. 164.
4. The phrase comes from a book of the same name by Phyllis Trible, *Texts of Terror: Literary Feminist Readings of Biblical Narrative*, SCM 1992.
5. A phrase used by Brigitte Kahl, 'Towards a Materialist–Feminist Reading' in *Searching the Scriptures*, Vol. 1, 236–9.
6. A point clearly made by Gail R. O'Day in her commentary on Acts in *The Women's Bible Commentary*, 305–12.

Chapter 13: Disbelieving Women

1. See, for example, Jane Schaberg on Luke in *The Women's Bible Commentary*, and Barbara Reid, *Women in the Gospel of Luke*, 198–204.
2. John Drury comments: 'The end of Mark's story is outside the text.' *The Literary Guide to the Bible*, edited by Robert Alter and Frank Kermode, Fontana Press 1987, 40.
3. Gabriel Josipovici, *The Book of God: A Response to the Bible*, Yale University Press: New Haven and London 1988, 258–60.

Epilogue: Knowing Her Place

1. From *The Complete Poems of Emily Dickinson*, edited by Thomas H. Johnson, Faber & Faber 1970, 1129.
2. Adrienne Rich, *The Dream of a Common Language*, W. W. Norton 1978/1993, 3.
3. *Swallowing a Fishbone: Feminist Theologians Debate Christianity*, edited by Daphne Hampson, SPCK 1996.
4. Nicola Slee, 'The Power to Remember' in *Swallowing a Fishbone*, 33–49.
5. Slee, op. cit., 46.
6. Mary Grey explores these paradoxes in *Beyond the Dark Night: A Way Forward for the Church?*, Cassell 1997.